Getting
What
You
Want
and Deserve

Getting What You Want

... from Rotten Bosses, Demanding Spouses, Phony Friends, Prying Parents, Annoying Neighbors, and Other Irritating People

and Deserve

MURIEL SOLOMON

Rutledge Hill Press®
Nashville, Tennessee
A Thomas Nelson Company

Published by Rutledge Hill Press, a Thomas Nelson Company, P.O. Box 141000, Nashville, Tennessee 37214.

Design by Harriette Bateman

Library of Congress Cataloging-in-Publication Data

Solomon, Muriel.
    Getting what you want (and deserve) : from rotten bosses, demanding spouses, phony friends, prying parents, annoying neighbors, and other irritating people / Muriel Solomon.
       p. cm.
    Includes index
    ISBN 1-55853-771-6
    1. Interpersonal communication. 2. Self-realization. I. Title.
    BF637.C45S634 1999
    158.2—dc21

                                                                99-41875
                                                                CIP

Printed in the United States of America
2 3 4 5 6 7 8 9—04 03 02 01 00

To Linda Burrows,
whose joyful spirit
taught me about courage

Contents

Part A — Professional Relationships 1

CHAPTER I. BOSSES 3

CHAPTER II. ASSOCIATES 27

Part B — Personal Relationships 119

CHAPTER VIII. SPOUSES AND SIGNIFICANT OTHERS 121

CHAPTER IX. YOUR EX 139

CHAPTER X. PARENTS 153

CHAPTER XI. TEENAGERS 169

CHAPTER XII. IN-LAWS AND OTHER RELATIVES 187

Part C — Additional Techniques to Deal with Infuriating Situations 229

Introduction

We lock horns with them everywhere. All those exasperating people make us feel angry, hurt, and frustrated. We find ourselves in infuriating situations with people such as:

- intimidating bosses
- meddling in-laws
- nagging spouses
- mud-slinging colleagues
- manipulative friends
- defiant teens
- haughty doctors
- obnoxious neighbors

I know you want to get back at the offenders who crush your ego. That's normal. I did, too, until I realized I was wasting a lot of energy. And worse, this misguided effort wasn't getting me where I wanted to go.

Once I figured out that strategic thinking and speaking allowed me to gain control over troublesome situations, I was able to help others. That's what this book is about.

Let's take Patricia as an example. When she came to me for help, she was secretary to an oppressive despot. "How could that tyrant be so mean to me?" she sobbed. "Whatever I do is wrong because he keeps changing his mind and then yelling at me, humiliating me in front of others. I can't take it anymore, but I need the job and I can't quit! What can I say to him?"

I told her that before she could answer that question, she needed to answer three other questions: What is your desired outcome? What strategy can make it happen? What steps are needed to implement your strategy? In a turn-around process of problem-solving, we worked backwards to develop the goal, strategy, tactics, and talk.

Patricia's goal was to stop being abused. Her strategy was to demand from her boss the respect due any worker while she looked into a transfer or work elsewhere. A new position might mean less pay, but she knew that daily fear and anxiety were putting her health at risk.

Confronting her boss was not as difficult as she feared. We rehearsed what she would say, along with appropriate body language. She told him that he had every right to criticize her work, but that he had no right to humiliate her in front of the staff. She also said that until she left she expected that both of them would be polite and act professionally. The bully, dumbfounded by her assertiveness, agreed. Things calmed down until she left a month later—with a letter of recommendation from her previously abusive boss!

Sometimes, as in Patricia's case, people are so stunned by the misery inflicted upon them that they can't get beyond the insult. However, it's important to listen carefully in order to *hear* what your tormentor wants. If you don't, you lose the chance to respond in a way that lets you achieve what you desire. Patricia told me that her boss was very proud of his professional achievements, so she challenged him to act professionally. Furthermore, I helped her to realize that she was dealing with a bully and bullies only respect those who stand up to them. In fact, showing backbone can actually turn some bullies into friends.

These are the types of situations you'll be reading about. Here you'll discover ways to get off your emotional merry-go-round by converting anger into creative energy. If you can state your goal clearly, you'll start exploring ways to achieve it. Then you can influence the outcome you're looking for. As you free yourself from manipulative webs spun by your opponents, you'll learn how to make others feel good about doing what you want done. You'll find new ways to confront people that not only resolve difficulties but can even transform them into golden opportunities.

This book is an instant-access resource for people problems. You don't have to read the entire book or a whole chapter to get assistance. The headings and subheadings in the contents give a quick overview of the topics you're seeking, with additional help from the index.

You won't find excessive verbiage or overanalysis. Just a distilled-to-the-essence guide to your goals and solutions. The mosaic of subjects was picked largely from questions posed to me by business associates, readers of my column and books, and listeners at my lectures, workshops, and media appearances. Of course, I haven't covered every conceivable situation, but from these you'll be able to master the process of dealing with new difficulties as they arise.

To assist you, you'll find strategies and scripts that I've developed over four decades of professional communication experience—writing, producing, motivating, teaching, and consulting. Assignments as diverse as training business executives to improve employee attitudes and productivity, educating employees about conflict resolution, working with the media on such topics as sex education, and assisting civic organizations to sensitize police officers, all helped me to prepare a concise, practical, and time-saving sourcebook.

I know this book can give you immediate relief. I hope it also gives you success in getting what you want and deserve.

—MURIEL SOLOMON

Part A

Professional Relationships

Don't just stand there with your mouth open, unable to speak, when business and professional people won't give you what they're supposed to. Raise hell! You can do that without shouting—politely and calmly letting them know you won't accept arrogant treatment.

From the time you could toddle, you've been taught to salute authority. Many of you still dread being thought disrespectful. So you let nasty bosses, teachers, doctors, and lawyers bamboozle you. Whether the power they have over you is real or imagined, you feel helpless, confused, bullied, and threatened.

When people you need in your everyday life take out their anger on you, they're often trying to overcome their own feelings of inadequacy. Actions of your workers or colleagues, clients or customers may be blatant or subtle. No matter. If they can make you feel fearful, they get the power they seek.

But you can gain the upper hand. Even with a boss who can fire you, a salesperson who does you a favor by talking to you, or a teacher who decides if you pass or fail, you can nevertheless feel in control.

Chapter I

Bosses

What can you say to a boss who must have learned torture from the Spanish Inquisition? Spying from the KGB? Whip-cracking from Simon Legree? Penny-pinching from Scrooge? Or scapegoating from the who-me politicians? *Plenty.*

And when you do, you'll regain self-respect. Especially in situations where the boss at a whim can have you demoted, fired, or black-balled. You'll master the fear of dealing with unfounded suspicions, deceitful accusations, unpredictable mood swings, and erratic rule enforcement. Even during those times when your own expectations are unrealistic, you don't have to feel trapped.

Chapter I gives you ways to break the stranglehold.

1. Spare the Ultimatum: Tell Me What You Want

Taming tyrants who freak out when displeased

You choke on resentment whenever your boss talks so loud all your colleagues and workers hear him call you Lamebrain. That's worse than his stern stare cutting through you like a laser.

Today you triggered a tirade when you questioned his decision affecting the project you manage. The boss refuses to hear opposing views on what he ought to do. This, he says, is crossing him and he makes you suffer by threatening to fire or demote you.

The insulting control freak verbally whacks away at your sense of security with his power club. You tolerate his abuse because you don't want to be fired. Meanwhile, he delights in scaring the hell out of you because he knows how much you need the job. You feel trapped.

THE GOAL
Get the boss off your back.
Be free from abuse without jeopardizing your position.

THE PLAN
1. *Develop a back-up action plan.* Relieve your fear of being fired by putting the *choice* of leaving or staying in your own hands. Topnotch performers no longer have lifetime guarantees. So update your resume, evaluate your abilities, and sharpen your skills. Ask your boss what else you should be learning and plan to acquire these needed special skills.

2. *Learn your current job market—just in case.* Scour journals, newspapers, and the Internet. Expand your personal network. Seek lunchtime and after-work job interviews without telling anyone in the office. It could get back to the boss and this might anger him even more.

3. *Document emotional abuse.* If you believe your boss lives to watch you squirm like a worm, ask personnel about a transfer or help from a counselor or ombudsman. Should you decide to leave, keep it friendly to protect your future.

4. *Let the boss vent his anger.* Keep quiet and he'll calm down quicker. Then if you ask questions *rather than defend your position*, a relentless tyrant won't keep pushing to break you just to prove he's right. To keep from coming unglued, concentrate on the results you want. If the rudeness continues, leave the room saying you'll return later.

5. *Listen intently to the answers and don't interrupt.* To show you understand *exactly* what's important to the boss, restate what he wants done or changed. Agree where you can; if you can't, acknowledge without arguing and suggest ways that you two, *acting as a team*, can help meet his goals and concerns.

6. *Change the way you challenge.* State your case, point by point. Rehearse a conversation at home, imagining your boss's problems and respecting his position. You're entitled to your opinion, but you don't have equal standing. Stick to the issue—it's the boss's action that's wrong, not the boss himself. If you show you're resentful, angry, and weak, the boss will peg you as inferior and dominate you even more.

7. *Disarm with the unexpected.* He expects you to submit. Surprise him and gain respect by maintaining strong, confident, pleasant body language. Grasping his reasoning and being firm and polite will shift the focus from blaming you to resolving the issue. Or you can let him retreat with an amused, "You're not really serious, are you?"

Solomon Says:

Try these three tips to slide the boss off your back:

- Straighten your spine. Bullies admire gumption.
- Ignore the results—pretend and speak as if you're a key member of the team.
- Show that tirades don't diminish your self-confidence.

THE SCRIPT

BOSS. [*winding down*]. You banana head. What a fiasco! I don't care what you think. I'm not going to let you cost me my career. We have to meet the deadline in the contract. It's your job to see supplies are delivered. They better be or else—

YOU. [*responding professionally, confidently, showing no emotion*]. I've been scouting the possibilities and here's the dilemma: Since the regular supplier can't deliver, a cheaper source can but it's a lower quality. If I get the promised quality from a more expensive source, we're eating into our profit. [*You have a solution but wait to tell it.*]

BOSS. Use the inferior brand. No one will know the difference.

YOU. [*disagreeing, you simply acknowledge*]. You think so? [*Put objections in form of questions.*] But wouldn't that be unethical?

BOSS. [*furiously—he perceived an implied insult*]. Look, you have to meet the deadline at the quoted price or you're outta here.

YOU. [*remaining calm, refocusing on the desired result*]. Hold on. Maybe we can work something out. [*Move to what we can do.*] What if I called the customers to explain the delay and let them choose between lower grade/cheaper rate or better quality/higher price? That would let us meet our deadline commitment and still keep the same profit margin.

BOSS. Good. You finally understand what I want.

YOU. [*smiling*]. I'm really glad. Boss, can we take a minute now to review this situation to avoid repeating a proce-dural problem? And I know you're not aware of this, but when you're screaming at me, I can't do my best work. So can we set some ground rules?

GUIDELINE
Tyrants revere toughies—let the blows bounce off.

Your confident thinking deserves the same respect you're willing to give your boss. The boss, too, looks for approval. Bullies crave respect.

2. SOS—
I'm Swamped

When excessive assignments are constantly dumped on you

Bosses aren't always *obviously* cruel and oppressive. A slick whipcracker tells you how great you are as she loads you down with her work. Asks you to pick up her houseplants because she doesn't want to dirty her own car. Or assigns you weekend duty because you don't have a family. You feel loyal, but you aren't her slave and resent her taking advantage and degrading your job.

Your trouble mushroomed after the company reorganized and people weren't replaced. Although given a new title, you had to combine responsibilities of another job with your own.

You don't know why you're being dumped on. You work better and faster than others and you do whatever is asked without mentioning it's not in the new job description. Perhaps the boss knows the work will get done without complaint. Or maybe she's punishing you for somehow offending her.

Regardless, you have to forget the *why* and move to the *what* to get this resolved. You can't work beyond your endurance or you'll become ill.

THE GOAL
Establish an equitable workload.

THE PLAN
1. *Consider why you get hooked.* If you've been falling for flattery or agreeing because you feel guilty, use a light touch to sandwich your refusal between two compliments.

2. *Assume your boss doesn't know she's Simon Legree.* Be friendly and state the problem calmly without blaming or whining. You've vented enough. Now prepare to face the issue.

3. *Ask your boss to spell out what's expected of you.* Ask her to set priorities and adjust time on other tasks when she gives you additional assignments. Speak up and set limits when you know you can't meet an unreasonable deadline without killing yourself.

4. *Suggest alternative procedures.* The boss may be clinging to an outdated, unworkable system. All organizations need innovative thinking—that could be your real value. Take the time to think through conditions, trends, and patterns. Do your own research to supply data showing how better workplace policies of similar companies have resulted in more dedicated and effective workers. Then seize the initiative, offer your ideas, and confirm your agreement in writing.

5. *Request your overtime be compensated.* If it's not in cash, then suggest increased benefits such as flextime, stock options, or telecommuting. Just be sure you're not honing and polishing when the boss simply wants the job done.

Solomon Says:

Three reasons you may be overworked:

- You're nursing a hurt instead of doctoring the problem—tell the boss you're suffering. A staff shortage is the boss's problem, not yours.

- You haven't suggested alternatives. And let go of tasks you can delegate, even if they won't be done as well.

- You haven't negotiated. Talk results—performance, not conformance. A more flexible schedule. Or more hours, more benefits.

THE SCRIPT

BOSS. Here's the proposed Warren contract. Check it out for me. Eugene, I can't do this without your help.

YOU. Thanks, boss. But as you're aware, I'm up to my ears in the conversion proposal. Which one do you want me to work on?

BOSS. We need both of them by the end of the week.

YOU. Aw c'mon, are you trying to make me feel guilty?

BOSS. Of course not. We're all doing more with less and everyone's stressed out.

YOU. Perhaps we could ease the tension and still keep the quality. We'd get better balanced work distribution if I could
train an assistant who'd always be available when I'm tied
up. We could have a team rotate non-job responsibilities
such as arranging events. And how about an incentive
chart, linking a bonus to productivity?

BOSS. Those are good ideas I'll consider. But this week, it looks
like you'll be working overtime—

YOU. OK, but don't you think it fair that my overtime be compensated? If you can't raise my salary, how about
increasing my insurance benefits or allowing me to work
from home one day a week?

GUIDELINE

Though you are neither chattel nor cattle, bosses don't get spoiled all by themselves.

Do you do more work than others simply because you've never questioned it?

3. Here's What I'm Worth; Let Me Tell You Why

Overcoming the fear of asking for a raise

Sometimes the oppression may be mainly in your head.

Your boss just has to look at you and you melt. Her icy stare zaps your courage. You think you deserve a raise, but you're scared to death to ask.

Certainly you've earned it. You're a hard worker, hardly ever miss a day even when you're sick. Who else has been so loyal? And your dedication always gets good performance evaluation ratings.

Besides, your wife keeps pestering you to talk to the boss. She's right about needing more money because expenses keep going up and your salary hasn't kept pace.

But what can you say to convince the boss? And how can you get over this numbing fear?

THE GOAL
Face your fear and learn where you stand.

THE PLAN
1. *Anticipate excuses.* Be ready with convincing responses. You may be told profits are down. That they're still restructuring and downsizing. That giving you a raise would create a domino effect or establish a poor precedent. Also, the boss may try to avoid a discussion, saying this isn't a good time.

2. *Consider reasons why raises are rejected.* In general, poor preparation. Focusing on the wrong reasons. Not collecting convincing evidence. Not rehearsing the presentation. Poor timing and not making an appointment. Lack of enthusiasm.

3. *Decide which options to request if there's no money.* An x-percent bonus if you produce y-amount within z-time, stock options, travel assignment, educational training, increased vacation time, and a flexible schedule are a few examples.

4. *Package proof of your achievements.* There's only one reason you deserve a raise: You made a valuable contribution to the organization and have the potential to continue contributing. Doing well—even doing very well—whatever is in your job description isn't enough to ask for a raise. Instead, recap your track record. Show how your accomplishments (additional responsibilities, improved department performance, increased x percent in sales, cut costs by $y) met those company needs. State how your skills will allow you to do even more in the future. Sell your worth without comparing it to anyone else.

5. *Rehearse your sales pitch.* Practice from bullet notes. Tape record yourself and play back, listening to your voice. Pretend you're the boss making objections, then respond to them. This drill lets you appear more relaxed, persuasive, and enthusiastic.

6. *Request a private meeting.* Aim for a time you're least likely to be interrupted. Ask the boss to please hold the calls and visits for a few minutes. Even if your knees are knocking, you can make yourself look and sound confident. You can be modest and still be assertive.

7. *Reinvent yourself for greater marketability.* After discussing what you have done, ask what the boss wants and how you can help in reaching her goals. What new functions or skills would increase your value? What training is available?

Solomon Says:

Prepare, or you're dead in the water. Three questions to answer:

1. Have I helped my company move ahead of the competition? Document and quantify how you improved product or service.

2. Have my responsibilities and productivity increased since my last raise? List specifics.

3. How does my salary compare with that for similar positions in other companies? What percentage raise do you expect?

8. *Use silence effectively.* After you give your pitch, shut up and give the boss a chance to mull it over. Being still is also a way to get the other person to start talking, even making concessions.

9. *Reduce a promise to writing.* Go back to your desk and write a succinct memo thanking the boss for her time and consideration and summarizing the discussion.

THE SCRIPT

YOU.   Thanks for making time for me. I'd like to brief you on some of the things we've been able to accomplish. When I finish, I'm convinced you're going to want to give me a raise. [*not one word about what you need*]

BOSS.   Look, if I give you a raise, it will start a stampede. We just can't afford increased salaries when profits are off.

YOU.   That's why you definitely need to reward your best worker now. Give me some incentive to keep working so hard. Just glance at these figures.

BOSS.   This is really impressive. I wish I could give you more, but we first have to increase our cash flow.

YOU.   Are you saying you need more customers who pay bills faster and more ways to reduce expenses?

BOSS.   Exactly.

YOU.   What if I came up with a plan that could help you do that? What if we could cut costs by a stated percentage in the next two months? Wouldn't that be worth an x-percent raise? I'd relish the challenge!

BOSS.   Well, I'd have to think about this.

YOU.   What would it take to make you accept my offer? You've nothing to lose. Is there any reason we can't agree on it?

GUIDELINE
Show how your talent meshes with your company's needs.
Don't request a raise until you can do this.

See also Chapter 80, "Overcoming the Fear of Approaching Your Boss."

4. Big Brother Is Watching and It's Disconcerting

When you're angry that the boss monitors your computer usage

Here's another area in which bosses are accused of abusing your rights.

You're bent out of shape because your boss acts like Agent Double-0-7. He contracted with a computer-spy company to look for lost hours on the Internet and who, when, and how each computer and phone extension is abused by personal use.

What's the big deal? There's a computer on every desk. When work is done in the allotted time, you feel free to tap into Yahoo or Games.com or send a social message. Now on top of all that your personal phone calls, voice mail, and e-mail are being bugged. And you're praying your boss hasn't seen your diatribe lampooning him in the e-mail you sent to a colleague.

With high-tech tools, you're at the mercy of the cyber patrol's prying eyes. You're sure being monitored (and maybe videotaped) while you're working tramples your rights. You and your colleagues are screaming, "Invasion of privacy!"

THE GOAL
Reach a reasonable snooping policy.

THE PLAN
1. *Calm down and review your position.* Demanding your right to use company equipment on company time doesn't give you a legal leg to stand on. These assets aren't purchased for personal enjoyment of workers.

2. *Assess the company's position.* As computer owners, employers don't need your knowledge or OK to review your e-mail. To protect trade secrets, they're entitled to see all messages inside the computers—including your critical memo. (You can delete, but you can't

hide. So be careful what you e-mail. Messages are usually stored in a back-up copy which would reveal your electronic fingerprints.)

3. *Learn why the policy exists.* Companies fear being held liable if there's a complaint, for example, that sexually harassing material was downloaded. They want to claim their policy prevents computer misuse.

4. *Pick out the policy flaws.* Your company, like many others, doesn't train workers in the proper use of the equipment or have written policies on usage and monitoring.

5. *Request sound and sensible changes.* To cut you some slack, convince your boss why it's in the company's interest to establish a fair, clear, and written policy. To secure the best work from the staff, everyone needs to know the limits of nonbusiness use of company equipment, and you and your boss need to trust each other.

Solomon Says:

Two rules for playing it safe:

1. Assume anything you say or write can come back to haunt you. Especially don't divulge information about your personal life.

2. Remember, you never know when someone you think is your friend may use this information against you.

THE SCRIPT

YOU. Boss, this computer spy thing has many of us feeling that we're being treated like kids.

BOSS. Then you should all behave more responsibly.

YOU. We understand you need to know if we goof off, just as we need to know what we can and can't do when we finish our work and need a break.

BOSS. Frankly, my main concern is not so much that you play games but that you waste computer memory. I have to be sure we'll always have enough available. If collected data show abuse of game options, I'll install the program that automatically erases them.

YOU. That's fair enough. But what about personal phone calls? Sometimes we need to call home to check on kids or get a repairman. The company needs us to work well, but how can we if we're worried about being monitored?

BOSS. It seems we need to establish some guidelines.

YOU. You're absolutely right. You know, you developed team spirit when you let us dress down on Fridays. It would also boost productivity if you'd let us relax a bit with the games. And everyone needs a little electronic privacy to deal with urgent problems or establish contacts.

BOSS. What are you suggesting?

YOU. Let us have a little while to talk without being spied on electronically. That would show you trust us to use our time wisely and still perform to your expectations. You set the limits. And we know you'll be fair.

BOSS. OK, I see your point. I'll prepare a policy memo on personal use of phones and computers.

Guideline
Persuade, don't push—dangle a desire.
To get the company to face up to formulating a policy, point out a way to the boss's wants rather than a demand of your rights.

5. I Was Only Trying to Help

Choosing between taking the initiative and being employed

At times, you're caught between the top brass and your yellow-bellied supervisor.

You discovered the check left by Mr. West for several items purchased was for an incorrect amount. After informing Chris, your supervisor, of your intent to work out the discrepancy with the customer, you phoned Mr. West and he agreed to send over the difference.

To your surprise, you were summoned to the front office and called on the carpet for violating company policy. Customer West had complained to your boss about your impudence.

You kept repeating you had permission from Chris to make the call and that the telephone conversation was cordial. Chris, to save her own skin, denied giving approval. The more you protested your innocence, the more the boss fumed. It was a case of you said/she said, and the boss believed Chris. Although you tried to do what you thought was right for the company, the boss said he'd let you know later in the day if you were to be fired.

THE GOAL

Keep your job.

THE PLAN

1. *Resist arguing and defending yourself.* Thinking you had a voice in decisions not yours to make was an unrealistic expectation. Participatory management means head honchos consider your ideas, but the one in charge makes policy decisions. You don't get to vote. Sure, the supervisor should have shown backbone and said you misunderstood each other. But when you're set up as the culprit, proclaiming your innocence only inflames. When it's your word against your supervisor's, the supervisor will be unscathed.

2. *Open your ears and close your mouth.* Sometimes telling the truth can bring threats of dismissal. You were so hell-bent on proving that you were right in the way you handled the situation, you didn't pick up on the boss's immediate worry—which is not your feelings or your vindication.

3. *Salvage what you can.* Review what was said to identify what is most important to your boss; namely, the reputation of the company and keeping customers happy. Concentrate on that until you can come up with an offer to improve the situation.

4. *Shift the emphasis.* Help emotions cool down. Right now all your angry boss is willing to hear from you is that you repent your sin. After acknowledging the blunder, move away from dwelling on it to taking some positive action to appease the customer. And since the manual didn't cover this particular situation, you can get back in good graces by suggesting a procedural change.

Solomon Says:

Do this if you trip on a bad or unclear rule:

- Try to get it changed to avoid a disaster.
- If you can't, follow procedures precisely to the letter.
- Maintaining that you did will abate the boss's anger and quickly effect change.

THE SCRIPT

BOSS. What kind of an upstart do I have working here? First you insult a very good customer and then you lie about getting the OK to do it.

YOU. I must have misunderstood Chris. I'm very sorry.

BOSS. Ryan, you don't even see what a terrible thing you did. I can't have every employee taking matters into his own hands. Not once did you apologize for violating company policy and offending Mr. West.

YOU. Boss, I do apologize. Obviously, I offended Mr. West. This was a dreadful misunderstanding and I'm extremely sorry he was upset. Although my intention was to protect the company, I now know I should leave that to those in a higher position.

Boss. Now I've got to placate West before he sounds off to others.

You. If you feel it would help, I could send a note to Mr. West taking full responsibility for the error, asking for his pardon, and enclosing a gift certificate which you can deduct from my salary.

GUIDELINE

Blame runs downhill. To save your job, choke down a little undeserved crow. Forget about absolution and make amends.

6. I Don't Intend to Play Your Blame Game

Protecting yourself when you're the scapegoat

Lugging unfair burdens goes back to ancient times. In those days a high priest transferred sins of the people to a goat and then drove it into the desert.

Today your boss, a school principal, has saddled his errors on your back, but you've no place to run. Though he's got your goat, you're not about to risk butting horns with your boss.

He sees you, as his assistant, as easy prey who can't or won't retaliate. Tells you what to do, then won't back you up. Uses weasel words so he can flip-flop later. When an order backfires, he denies giving it. Holds you responsible without giving you authority to make decisions.

This gutless creature is too scared to take a risk or take a stand or take action even in a crisis. You can't get a straight answer and you can't trust what he does say.

You're walking on eggshells. Will your professional standing be hurt by his finger pointing? Claiming his hands are clean, your retro advisor boss tells you what you should have done—when it's too late. Then he attacks you personally. Bushwhacked and ambushed, you're hit without warning and left to survey the damage.

THE GOAL
Combine fair treatment with career protection.

THE PLAN
1. *Anticipate and avert potential danger.* Move to change procedures. When accepting a new assignment, ask questions that make the boss spell out his expectations. Know your scope of responsibility and which orders the boss will be giving.

2. *Hoist your antenna.* Pay attention to office politics when colleagues talk about difficult bosses. Find allies to back you up and join forces.

3. *Record your actions as you proceed.* Protect yourself with copies to others involved. If some uncomplimentary statement gets in your personnel file, write your own response to accompany it.

4. *Convince the boss to hold regularly scheduled meetings, if he isn't already doing so.* Even if it's just for a few minutes a week to check bases and stay on track. Pin down any general criticism (e.g., "bad attitude") into specific charges.

5. *Collect information.* Finding items helpful to the boss can win him over.

Solomon Says:

When bosses protect their hides, it won't get under your skin if you:

- Obtain more than a verbal OK from now on.

- Fight back without inflicting wounds—don't accuse or personalize.

- Supply answers to the boss's current dilemma. This makes you practically indispensable.

THE SCRIPT

PRINCIPAL.   How did you let this item get in the morning newspaper?

YOU.   Gee, boss, I guess you forgot the agreement we had that I wouldn't talk to the media. [*Don't accept his blame; toss it back politely, with a friendly tone.*] You said only the principal should speak for the school.

PRINCIPAL.   I am holding you personally responsible for this mess. When the reporter said a parent complained about the treatment her child received, you should have issued a denial when I wasn't here to do it.

YOU.   [*Don't tell him he's wrong.*] Maybe so, but I see it another way. If I did that, wouldn't I be breaking the rules? But about this situation, would you like me to draft a statement you can call in?

PRINCIPAL. Yes, get right on it.

YOU. I know we both want a smooth operation, so how do we keep this from happening again? You have every right to criticize my performance, but don't you think you were being unnecessarily rough? I'm trying to adhere to the rules. This points up a need to amend our current rules of procedure.

GUIDELINE

Quickly defuse any grenades tossed at you. Quote chapter and verse of the boss's own rules along with an offer to help.

See also Chapter 82, "Lowering Hostility by Retrieving the Right Words"

7. It's a Mistake, but It Didn't Merit the Riot Act

Responding to a tongue-lashing you didn't deserve

It hardly seems fair that some bosses read you the riot act over minor matters.

OK, you shaved the truth a tiny bit, and now you can't imagine how the little white lie mushroomed into a cover-up. The fib boomeranged when you claimed to have already taken care of a complaint, which you hoped would die a natural death, but it came back to haunt you.

It wasn't really as bad as it seems. Mrs. Corona is a pain, always finding fault with something. You told her you had reordered when you hadn't actually. You were waiting to send in her corrected order with the next batch.

But Mrs. Corona called again, and the boss checked the orders and found you weren't being forthright. Although your job is on the line, you're still stonewalling. You don't think what you did is so terrible. Defiantly, you issued an insincere apology.

Now your boss is raving mad. Outside of rending your clothes and getting down on your knees, what can you do to smooth things over?

THE GOAL

Rebuild the trust and respect you've lost.

THE PLAN

1. *Admit your misjudgment head-on.* Before you're caught. Denials are tricky to master and should be used judiciously only when you're innocent. You'd have been better off saying the devil made you do it. You can't defend the indefensible. From now on, own up instantly, sincerely, and emphatically.

2. *No excuses, just suggest how you'll fix the problem.* Don't blame others or back-peddle with, "It wasn't my fault." Or sound insincere with, "If I offended. . ."

3. *Control your guilt.* Don't go overboard. Maintain a professional manner and tone. Stay calm. Look directly at your boss. Speak up slowly and carefully without any uhs and ums.

4. *Soothe the feelings you've trampled on.* Empathize with the pain the other person feels you caused.

5. *Accept deserved penalties without wiggling out.* This allows you to appear strong rather than weak and sniveling, searching for a scapegoat. Be gracious about paying for the damage in whatever form that may take.

6. *Move on, rising above the accusations.* Suggest how to repair or prevent a repetition of the problem.

Solomon Says:

Whoa! To consider whether the boss or you may be right:

- First, listen without arguing. Don't alibi even if the boss shares blame for the blunder.

- Admit your part with a sincere apology.

- Then quickly suggest how to repair the damage.

THE SCRIPT

YOU. If Mrs. Corona misunderstood me, I'm sorry [*sounds obviously insincere*].

BOSS. Not taking responsibility for the boner, more than the mistake itself, infuriates me.

YOU. I didn't think she'd know the difference.

BOSS. You stupid oaf! She is one of our best customers. You offended her. We'll not only lose *her* business but that of all the others she's able to influence. How could you be so dense!

YOU. Yes, I see now that was a really stupid thing to do. I screwed up. I mishandled the situation. And I'm terribly sorry for my lack of good judgment.

Boss. Well, I don't know how we're going to get out of this problem you created.

You. I'd like to suggest that we rush the order. In the meantime, I'll find a local supplier and personally deliver enough until the rush order comes through. Since this is my fault, I'll pay for the additional costs and it will give me a chance to apologize face-to-face with the customer.

GUIDELINE
Apologies that aren't heartfelt are worse than no apologies at all.

8. Do You Mind If I Put That in Writing?

When your boss habitually backs out of a promise

Talk about unfair! What about the boss who keeps building up your hopes, then smashing them? Working for your buddy-buddy boss is no bed of roses.

You believe now that the boss never intended to keep his promises. Maybe he later realized he didn't have the authority to carry them out. Or perhaps he's so streaked with yellow that he can't say no to your face, and will promise you anything he thinks you want.

Whatever the motive, you feel used. You're kicking yourself for being so naive. You'd really like to confront him for keeping you hanging on to a promise and then disappointing you. But if you ask him about reneging on your deal, he'd only claim that you reached the wrong conclusion. His ambiguity is underhanded.

His latest monkey wrench was promising to support you for an upcoming appointment. Rather than tell you he had to protect his position by withdrawing support, he left you twisting in the wind.

What a thin-skinned phony. How can you ever believe him again when he flirts with the truth—or deserts it—by acting so irresponsibly?

THE GOAL
Induce the boss to keep a promise.

THE PLAN
1. *Move beyond a handshake.* To safeguard your interests, get your agreement in writing and send copies to all other relevant parties. Without a signed agreement, it's the boss's word against yours. Even with a signed agreement, the boss may find loopholes.

2. *Consider the source.* If the boss objects to a written agreement or says you misunderstood in your summarizing memo, you have no promise. It's like an empty safe-deposit box, so stop banking on it.

3. *Make the benefits mutual.* Stress how the boss will benefit also from the proposed agreement. Your interests converge when you focus on the same goal.

Solomon Says:

Three steps to tactful confronting:

1. If you say you assume a misunderstanding, this lets you question without accusing.

2. After you're given a promise, prepare a written agreement—what the boss needs, what you get in return. Circulate copies to others involved.

3. Include a reminder of what's in it for the boss who follows through—a problem solved, a goal reached, etc.

THE SCRIPT

YOU.   Let me see if I have this straight. As long as I continue the same steady reduction in operating costs for the next three months, you are going to recommend my promotion.

BOSS.   Yes, of course.

YOU.   Then you won't mind if I put this agreement in writing to be certain there's no misunderstanding later on. I know you have good intentions, but frankly, I've been disappointed in the past and I don't want to get my hopes up while I'm putting in a lot of extra effort.

BOSS.   Oh, a written agreement isn't necessary. We understand each other.

YOU.   Yes, I think we finally do. [*You know he'll weasel out again unless you come up with some lure.*] As an added incentive for both of us, I'll prepare a breakdown you can brag about in your quarterly report to the district office.

GUIDELINE
Be ankle-deep in the reneger's incentive before you hold his feet to the fire.

Chapter II

Associates

Chapter II covers a variety of ways to feel miserable—dealing with workers who can't do, won't do, are unpredictable, get mad, or get others in trouble. Nevertheless, you need these subordinates because the work they do affects your own performance.

Ideally, each member should feel privileged to be part of your team. Some feel so privileged due to their high production, they strut around like royal peacocks too important to do required routine. Others cause despair with their unexpectedly poor performance. Another headache comes from the snitch. If the information is accurate you can use it, but you suspect you're being manipulated by a spiteful troublemaker.

Then there's the disgruntled worker who can infect others and cause morale to plummet. Some are so well liked that if you reprimanded them, their coworkers would raise the roof. When it's necessary to fire someone, employers today carefully weigh potential consequences. Among other problems, workers could become violent if this action isn't handled carefully and with sensitivity.

9. I Think We Need to Come to an Understanding

Bringing into line challengers to your authority

Good workers who deliberately disobey your orders are terribly infuriating.

You've been with the company for quite a while and recently transferred to another branch as the new manager. One of your specific tasks was to upgrade existing systems.

Kevin is openly opposing your changes. He works hard but refuses to do what you want in the new way you want it done. He keeps using the old system, which isn't designed to elicit the exact data you need for decision-making.

He's too good and experienced to fire, but you're angry at having to keep explaining yourself. Kevin's attitude wastes your time and you feel like you're a pressure cooker about to blow.

Today he was guilty of insubordination by contradicting you three times in front of customers. You swallowed your anger, trying to figure out what you could do to turn him around.

THE GOAL

Reduce resistance by gaining cooperation.

Stop the bold resistance and improve performance to avoid high turnover cost.

THE PLAN

1. *Review the assignment.* Kevin needs to know how his job relates to the whole operation and the company goals. Maybe his defiance stems from lacking the necessary know-how to do things your way, the new way, rather than from resistance to change. Make yourself or another worker accessible to hear a problem he can't solve on his own.

2. *Reexamine your directives.* Studies show workers need more back and forth communication. A dialogue gives them a voice in decisions affecting their work even though you have the final say. Employees can't read your mind—maybe you've impatiently dismissed questions, discouraging clarification. Keep orders simple. Spell out what you want done, why, in what form, by when, who else is involved, and accountabilities. Schedule regular feedback-guidance sessions to acknowledge what's good and to suggest where to improve.

3. *Let the defiant one keep his dignity.* What comes out as insubordination is usually unresolved frustration. If you attack him before others, you wound his pride and make a lifetime enemy. Being right doesn't entitle you to ridicule him. When you focus on the act, not the person, you avoid saying, "You're wrong." Instead, criticize by stating facts and reviewing consequences.

4. *Utilize ad hoc committees.* Let other workers assist you with a problem worker. This shifts the problem from boss-employee to a work group issue. A major motivator is the desire to gain peer approval and not to disappoint fellow workers or teammates. Encourage peer support and recognition.

THE SCRIPT

YOU. Kevin, we need to have a little talk. Is there something you want to tell me, some problem here? [*He already knows he was wrong to embarrass you in front of customers. You don't have to tell him that—you do need to hear why he did it.*]

KEVIN. You're not doing things the way Mike did. I don't like the way you're running this place. [*Let him get it all out without interrupting*]

YOU. Yes, I have made some changes and I know new ways take some getting used to. However, each change was one that benefits the company. The more profit we make, the more secure your job. That's the way it's going to be from now on.

KEVIN. Are you going to write me up in the personnel file?

YOU. No, I think we now understand each other. I'm confident you'll be able to follow the new rules. If I'm wrong, then I will have to put a future incident in your file.

YOU. Kevin, I want to talk to you about the reports you keep handing me using the old forms. Haven't I made it clear that I need data in a newly designed way?

KEVIN. I'm sorry, boss.

YOU. I don't want an apology. I want you to tell me what the problem is with the new form. [*No accusation, the focus is on the problem.*]

KEVIN. The new form requires a sophisticated knowledge of statistics. Frankly, I don't know how to make those computations and I was too embarrassed to tell you. I thought you got what you needed the old way, but I guess I was wrong.

YOU. Yes, after I explain why that change is important, I'll see that you get the training you need.

GUIDELINE

Leave the defiant with a choice of consequences.

Rather than issue a my-way-or-you're-out-of-here ultimatum that could evoke angry retaliation, extend an option that invites cooperation.

10. Let's Pull on the Same End of the Rope

Getting prima donnas to do what's required

Another defiant group is the office royalty.

Babs is a fine worker, almost irreplaceable, who wants to run the show her way. Her ideas are very good—but she lies and manipulates to avoid your orders. Prolonged talks and ordered counseling haven't helped. You've been putting up with a lot of her shenanigans—particularly her moving on her own when your OK is needed.

Because she brings in the most business, this rainmaker presumes she's entitled to break the rules. She gets temperamental if interrupted and won't be bothered with deadlines and routines she feels are beneath her.

She won't, for example, train junior associates or attend planning meetings with colleagues, which are part of her duties. Babs struts around the office, mounts pictures of herself with large donors, and anyone within earshot knows her latest tally.

Other competent workers resent having to do what Babs doesn't get done. Some have left because they object to special treatment given prima donnas. How can you control this offensive behavior?

THE GOAL

Keep your money-makers producing while reducing the dissension.

THE PLAN

1. *Reassert your rules.* Of course, those who must adhere to your regulations become discontented or angry when you indulge wrongdoing by one person.

2. *Protect yourself.* Acting without required permission must be nipped in the bud. It sets a dangerous precedent. You'll find yourself held accountable for an act done without your knowledge.

3. *Counsel the prima donna.* Explain why she'll benefit more by revising her attitude around the office.

4. *Find new ways to reward the rainmaker.* Yes, you feel beholden to office royalty who bring in the most clients, but stop being so obvious in showing favoritism. You can encourage her with benefits that don't interfere with *daily* operations.

5. *Use additional motivators.* Organizations that report a low rate of turnover encourage company loyalty by providing a wide variety of incentives. Many examples of these are discussed in Chapter 83, "Reducing Worker Frustration with Effective Policies."

Solomon Says:

Five tips for working with temperamentals:

1. Hold firm. They're like kids, trying to bend your rules until they break. Show they can't take advantage of your easygoing style.

2. Call their bluff. No one's indispensable. Regain respect with consistent enforcement.

3. Explain the advantages to adhering, the consequences for disobeying rules.

4. Have them describe the troublesome behavior needing change to be sure they understand the problem.

5. Agree to how the changes will happen.

THE SCRIPT

YOU. Babs, we're going to have to make some changes around here. Morale is in a slump because the staff complain about unfair distribution of labor.

BABS. I keep clients happy because they get top service. Besides being extremely knowledgeable and able to make good recommendations, I pay close attention to their needs. It's their satisfaction that brings us new clients.

YOU. And we appreciate your contributions, Babs. However, I want to explain to you why it's necessary that everyone follow our rules. First, why you have to get my permission in situations where you know it's required [*tough, fair, non-accusatory*]. Suppose, without your knowing it, your worker negotiated a deal that backfired and you were called on the carpet. You're responsible without the slightest excuse. What would you do?

BABS. I guess I'd be pretty ticked off.

YOU. Exactly. I know I won't have to mention this to you again. Now about your taking part in planning and training—

BABS. I'm sorry some people think I'm shirking, but I need leeway to do what I do best and give this company what it needs.

YOU. We won't have a company left for you to help if others resent your special privileges. Being brilliant isn't enough to rise to the top. Don't let bad behavior limit your career growth. However, I do want to show you my appreciation for your efforts. In return for your increased team spirit and cooperation with office routine, I am willing to offer you additional benefits that I'm sure will keep you happy.

GUIDELINE
Favoritism poisons morale.

When you cater to office royalty, expect to be crowned with complaints and a peasant revolt.

11. Make Peace, Not War

*When feuding workers
go on the warpath*

During these downsizing decades, old-time two-way company loyalty has disappeared. Now your best workers know that while jobs aren't permanent, their skills are portable and will go with them when they leave. Today the desire to control one's career is stronger than money and incentive rewards.

So as a manager in a fast-growing field, you're faced with a shortage of skilled workers. Everyone feels stress and strain. People are quick to anger and some pick fights.

Take Bradley, a transferred division director, who's had several run-ins with colleagues. He goads other directors and stirs up workers. This is a big factor in cooperation among divisions sinking to a new low. Employees are taking sides. Accusations are flying back and forth, placing blame on the foul-ups. Bradley's people, though, remain supportive.

In this tense atmosphere, Bradley reluctantly agreed on a plan for cross-training. He hasn't followed through, probably because he'd have to meet with the other directors. It would take too long to find a replacement for Bradley. You know, however, that you must take some action or the situation can only continue downhill.

THE GOAL
Rebuild morale by bringing a troublesome worker back in line.

THE PLAN
1. *Move quickly and prepare for the future.* If you made a bad appointment choice you can't correct now, don't wait until your ship sinks to search for a potential replacement. Not to be caught short, some companies require all supervisors to train their successors.

2. *Privately encourage the rebel to express his hostility.* Put the blame on the plan that appears not to be working. Ask for his opinion. Your friendly questions will get him to tell you why he didn't do his part to implement the plan.

3. *Meet individually with your other division directors.* Acknowledge that everyone is upset. Open the communication door and brace yourself for complaints. Since these managers already know the exasperating issue, cut them off by asking for their help with the problem before they bring it up.

4. *Now you're ready for regularly scheduled meetings.* Beyond the clash of personalities, look at a system that can be improved. Also consider ways to interject some fun that would ease the anger and tension from overwork stress.

Solomon Says:

Three tactics that can reduce tension:

1. Make each worker feel special. Talk to them as people, not robots. Give earned praise, acknowledging areas of expertise and sharing credit for your unit's success.

2. Ask about their personal concerns and interests. Show you care by fighting for their rights.

3. Be a kind critic. Let them save face while helping them. ("I know you're trying. Maybe if you did it this way instead.")

THE SCRIPT

BRAD. You wanted to see me, boss?

YOU. [*at the end of the day when most employees have left*]. Yes, about the cross-training plan. I thought it would give us more flexibility and relieve some stress. But we can't get it off the ground. What do you think is the trouble? Please feel free to be frank.

BRAD. I think you're expecting the impossible. We don't have the time for this and still keep up with our regular work. Cross-training only slows us down and makes us work harder.

YOU. How do you think we could get around that problem? What would it take?

• • •

YOU. [*to your division directors*]. We apparently have a problem with poor communication and cooperation among our divisions. I need your thinking on the best ways to improve the situation. After all, you do the jobs and you have ideas on how to fix what's wrong.

GUIDELINE

Preserve dignity and reduce resentment—let employees take part in decisions affecting their work.

12. We Have a Conflict, So Let's Try to Resolve It

Dismissing an unpredictable, potentially dangerous saboteur

An employer today has to be especially delicate when firing a worker.

Bennett was enraged over a few of your business decisions. When he felt you didn't listen to him, he took these as a personal affront and has been simmering ever since. Threatening to get even, he's a potential danger to you and your operation.

With his fine-tuned knowledge of computer systems, Ben could erase vital data or substitute wrong information or destroy equipment. He could make a deliberate mistake for which you'd be blamed. He might even level charges against you to higher-ups or the media.

You know instinctively he can no longer be trusted and want to fire him. If you do fire him for being disruptive and noncompliant, would he come after you and his fellow workers? With so many reports of fired workers returning to the workplace and committing violent attacks, threats by angry workers must be taken seriously.

THE GOAL
Reduce the anger of an about-to-be-fired employee.

THE PLAN
1. *Show sensitivity when disagreeing.* Whether you're turning down a personal request or a proposal, or overriding opinions, or firing an employee, there's no need to be abrasive or humiliating. Keep your words and your facial expression pleasant. When you don't correct what a (up to now) good employee feels is troublesome, his expectations may be unrealistic. The problem may be miscommunication rather than mistreatment.

2. *Reduce tension by going over your personnel policies.* Be up front so that everyone understands what to expect. To let workers know you're being fair and equitable, consider providing conflict resolution training along with a crisis plan (e.g., allow going to a higher-level-management or a peer-review panel). Offering severance pay and help with job training and placement when you have to let people go will relieve some stress.

3. *Update your security.* Do you rotate passwords and security codes for your computers? Do you need to install cameras?

4. *Keep your word.* Don't promise unless you're sure you can deliver. People become very angry when they see a boss-reneging pattern, promises broken with, "You must have misunderstood me." Deep resentment can lead to revenge as well as embarrassment to everyone involved.

5. *Fire with caution.* Document your actions, starting with your verbal warning about job performance, followed by a written one if the problem continues. Be sure you can't be accused of discrimination. Do the firing privately not to humiliate the worker, being clear about the reason and without any more discussion.

THE SCRIPT

YOU. [*a kind, diplomatic refusal*]. Your idea is (good) (worth considering) but because of other commitments, I can't use it at this time. It's a shame because the value is in using it now while that topic is on the front burner.

• • •

YOU. Ben, I understand your objection to the policy; however, I believe if you had all the facts, you'd see why that decision was made. Let me enlighten you. Here's the scoop and the bottom line. . .

BEN. But this isn't fair. I feel I've been exploited. It's a stupid way to handle it and I won't go along. Not only that, I'm letting others know what's going on here.

YOU. Look, Ben, I can see that you're still upset, but making threats doesn't resolve anything. Let's go over this once more and—

BEN. It's no use. This is not what you promised. No one listens to me around here. I'll find a way to make you see how wrong you are.

YOU.   Ben, I'm sorry we can't work this out. I'm cautioning you to focus on the consequences of your actions. Consider this a warning. If you don't comply, you'll be saying good-bye to your job here.

• • •

YOU.   Ben, as we've discussed during your probation, your failure to comply with company policy and your defiant attitude have resulted in your dismissal. Please write your comments on this termination report *[that keeps an employee from switching stories at a later time]*. Good luck to you.

GUIDELINE
Make the firing process civil, precise, and concise.

13. No One Likes a Tattletale

*Querying informers
who may be malicious troublemakers*

You're all but choking on suspicious air. As a manager, it's important that you know what's going on.

Ed comes to you with information and you're wondering if he's seeing things that aren't there. Is he using you to stir up trouble? Is he an overly zealous competitor trying to appear more important than another worker, or is he just trying to gain Brownie points?

As much as you hate the idea of someone snitching, you need to hear the news. But Ed's stories may or may not be true because he seems delighted to disparage a colleague allegedly caught in wrongdoing. And it's to his advantage to tell you that his rival Mac has been negating company policy by harassing women, whether or not that's accurate.

However, if this is true and you have knowledge of alleged misbehavior, looking the other way would get you in hot water. You need some sort of policy for handling informants and the information they give you.

THE GOAL
Unclog communication and verify tall tales.

THE PLAN
1. *Regard snitches as rumormongers.* Track down the rumor or complaint. Don't assume anything—you have to know if the information is the truth, embroidery, distortion, or flat-out lie because you're held responsible. Learn if the problem could have serious consequences requiring immediate action or a change in procedures. Or is this spiteful gossip from a squealer with something to gain by bringing you the juicy tidbit?

2. *Let team partners work out their own personal problems themselves.* Don't play peacemaker—it's their responsibility. You can, however, offer to set up a meeting for the two to sit down and work it out. When squealing doesn't bring about the desired result, it will stop.

3. *To get news, open your door; to spread news, feed the grapevine.* Set a day and time for your people to come by without appointment. Although spies get immediate access to your office, all of you need feedback and workers need your reassurance. Get out of your office to mingle. Stop by different desks, ask questions, sense the general feeling, and be alert to potential problems. Pump in selected information you want spread. People rely on the grapevine to learn what's happening.

4. *Continually update information to your group.* That's the best way to control the spread of misinformation. For example, establish a rumor hotline or put a dependable person in charge of maintaining an attractive and accurate bulletin board.

THE SCRIPT

ED.   I thought you'd want to know that Mac's been harassing Amanda lately.

YOU.   This surprises me, Ed. I've never before had to question Mac's behavior. [*You're wondering what he has to gain by bringing you this juicy tidbit.*] What exactly did Mac say or do? Did you actually observe this?. . .Then how did you hear about it?. . .Do you know who told it to Abby?

• • •

YOU.   Amanda, I'm glad you came in. It was told to me that one of the guys has been harassing you. If this is true, you have my word that I'll put a stop to it without your saying anything publicly. But I need accurate information. Did anyone behave unprofessionally toward you, and if so, who did and what was said or done?

• • •

YOU.   Mac, I'm tracing a rumor. Can you confirm any behavior that could be construed as sexual harassment? [*Mac admits making crude remarks to Amanda.*] Your work is good, but you are hereby on notice that kind of language will not be tolerated in this office. I'm putting this account in your record. A second offense and you'll be leaving us.

• • •

YOU. [*at your staff meeting*]. I have set aside a block of time, every Thursday from three to five, when I hope you'll feel free to stop by to discuss any problem. I don't like surprises. It's come to my attention that some of you aren't fully aware of the meaning of sexual harassment in the workplace and the legal consequences for a company if this takes place. Let's discuss the issue and then I want your thinking on how potential problems can be prevented.

GUIDELINE

Be abundantly clear that you want your workers to tell you about potential problems.

Even if you have to put up with rumors or snitching, you can quickly separate these from real trouble that needs correcting.

Chapter III

Colleagues

Your workplace is polluted. Constant tension fills the air, feeling as deadly as noxious gas, when fights involve personalities.

If the arguing were over issues or procedures, fine. Ideas have to compete or we'd never make any progress. This can result in the best ideas surviving. But people problems are different. These fester unless the personality conflicts are treated.

Many problems between colleagues or coworkers stem from a misguided desire to push another down in order to appear more important. Or a colleague believes the workload isn't equitable. Others upset coworkers with unrelenting criticism, backbiting, belittling, and sneak attacks. They'd rather undermine their work than confront them.

This chapter deals with ways to handle the trouble without stooping to the troublemaker's tactics.

14. Say It to My Face or Not at All

*Confronting backstabbers
and gaining their respect*

You can't let malicious, behind-your-back comments about your work go unchecked.

In Al's game of nasty politics, he produces more myths than the ancient Greeks. Al always acts friendly to your face, but you've heard from several sources that he's been ripping you apart. It's a cheap shot. You're not there to defend yourself when he's spreading lies about you and your work.

You think Al's super ego is driving him to promote himself by cutting you down. He's obviously trying to show his superiority to the boss and your colleagues, taking over at the slightest opportunity.

You'd like to tell Al, "Look, generalisimo, who appointed you commander?" But you've been holding back. Now you're ready to punch him out.

THE GOAL

Institute damage control.
And, if possible, win over your opponent.

THE PLAN

1. *Pause and plot.* Of course, you're angry. You feel like you were stabbed, but take a deep breath, count to ten, and slowly exhale the emotion. Let your anger work for you instead of against you. Give yourself time to simmer down and regain your professionalism. Al's method was nasty, but his message may have a grain of truth you can use.

2. *Rehearse what you'll say.* Remember Al is just another bully, expecting you to react emotionally. You want to appear firm and in control. Keep your confrontation private, direct, and face-to-face.

3. *Substitute "I" for the accusatory "you."* You'll make more progress from, "I'd appreciate hearing your complaints directly," than from, "You're a snake in the grass for going behind my back."

4. *Question your adversary.* Pull out the specifics about his complaints and ask him for possible solutions.

5. *Disarm with an honest compliment.* Your critic was expecting you to counterpunch. Instead, throw him off guard. This helps especially when you suspect your adversary's problem is envy.

Solomon Says:

You can win either way by confronting:

- If your nemesis denies backstabbing, you've probably prevented a repeat performance.

- If the backstabber owns up to the charge, you've created the chance to work out the problem together. In the future, you won't have to talk through a third party.

THE SCRIPT

AL.   Hi, good to see ya. How's everything?

YOU. Al, we need to talk. I've been hearing some upsetting things. I realize it's uncomfortable for both of us to be talking about disagreements, but can we hash this out without putting on boxing gloves? Do you think we can drop the pretense and talk about the problem?

AL.   I don't know what you're referring to.

YOU. I'm talking about reports that you're telling everybody I mishandled the case and how you would have handled it better.

AL.   Why are you getting so touchy?

YOU. [*with a teasing smile*]. Because if that's so, you know that's not the way we do things around here. You have good ideas, Al, and I'd appreciate your thinking. But you had your chance to voice your comments and criticism in the group meeting. I'd have been glad to explain my actions then. Are you willing to tell me now face-to-face what you're so concerned about?

AL. So I said a few things out of line. Big deal.

YOU. When you say things like that it appears that you'd rather fight than resolve this matter. I really don't want to fight with you and prefer to disagree professionally. But if you embarrass me like that again, I'll have a shock for you at the next meeting. [*This is no idle threat. If he continues, you'll expose Al's antics.*]

GUIDELINE

Hand the backbiter a threat he won't forget.

Confront with promised consequences. But keep him guessing and the bully will probably refrain from stabbing you in the back again.

15. Don't Even Think about Sandbagging Me Again

Handling an underhanded
surprise attack in front of others

While backbiters take advantage of your absence, snipers bank on your presence to enhance their attacks.

Samantha set you up to look stupid in front of the boss. You never saw it coming. You've been trying to ignore this colleague who's been giving you trouble, who does anything to make you feel inferior or undermine your credibility.

Now you need to rebound or the boss will think you're incapable of getting up after being floored. You can't afford to turn the other cheek when you work with mean, contemptible, tricky, phony, exploitive manipulators.

Samantha's attacks are brazen. Instead of sniping under cover, she strikes during a group setting. The darts are thinly disguised. Some have sly wording or supposed humor to immobilize your reaction. If it looks as though you're going to take offense, she beats you to it with "only kidding." Except you know it was deliberate.

So far you've refrained from counterattacks, but you're afraid the unfair accusations will damage your reputation.

THE GOAL
Seize control of the discussion when verbally attacked.

THE PLAN
1. *Verify that you are being attacked.* Check your assumption by asking the sniper to clarify the real or imagined insult. Snipers and hecklers often back down at this point. When you find you've been sandbagged, say you're happy to discuss any legitimate criticism. Ask her to be specific about why your idea won't work.

2. *Prepare in advance for these sessions.* Since you know what's coming, you can be ready with pertinent facts at your fingertips. You can

ask her for her opinion *before* the meeting on an item you plan to present. Act friendly and confident as you look her in the eye and stand erect refuting false information and impressions.

3. *When alone, ask if you've offended the sniper.* If so, apologize; if not, say you felt offended and attacked although you assume it was not intentional.

4. *Show you can get along well with others.* Samantha may have powerful friends higher up in the company. Be a team player. After all, you don't have to like people to work well with them.

5. *See beyond your immediate project.* You're going to need cooperation from colleagues who don't report to you. To protect your career, identify the lateral relationships you'll need and the people capable of blocking your goals. Seek their advice from the start so that (a) they'll buy into a plan in which they have a vested interest and (b) the plan itself will be improved by knowledgeable input.

THE SCRIPT

SAM. *[at the staff meeting]*. Can you tell us why your project is running so much over budget? According to these figures—

YOU. I'm afraid you've been given wrong information. The facts you've stated are not accurate. I have here an updated accounting.

SAM. Are you saying you are not running over budget?

YOU. We're pretty much on target. I don't want to waste everybody's time by going over the details. I've submitted my report and, Samantha, I'll be glad to set you straight after the meeting.

YOU. *[in private]*. Samantha, did I imagine it or were you attacking me at the meeting?

SAM. No attack. I just wanted more information.

YOU. I'm glad that's all it was. But I have to say I found the cutting remarks offensive. I'm sure you won't be doing that to me any more.

GUIDELINE
When bitten by a snake, don't let the venom penetrate.
Toss back your responses without appearing rattled.

16. Hold Your Fire—
We Need to Work Together

*When rivals spread rumors
or sling mud at you*

Your competitor's attacks have become so severe, you're calling him "the Terminator."

You don't remember how it all began, but for the past year you and George have been rivals. Everything with him is a contest he has to win regardless of the means. He's more into tying you up in knots than in unraveling the problems on your project.

George sees you as a threat to his influence with the boss. Believing that all's fair in war and getting ahead, he tells his tall tales to gain a competitive edge. Then he goes around the office, one-on-one, informing anybody who'll listen how you've managed to botch up your job.

The mud George throws is hurting your reputation. In fact, he appears determined to destroy it. If his neck wasn't so dirty, you'd wring it. How can you expose his motives and control his verbal sabotage?

THE GOAL
Help restore a friendlier atmosphere.

THE PLAN
1. *Keep mum until your goal is clear.* First you have to think through what you want to accomplish and what you can actually control.
2. *Take the high road.* You can only guess at your opponent's motives and knowing them won't really help you. Appear willing to help solve problems, not like your rival who's stuck in the mud. Inflammatory language boomerangs. Sling back, and not only will the mud splatter on you, but you'll also find a chorus of critics turning on you.
3. *Go face-to-face.* Electronic or written memos can be misinterpreted. When a matter needs to be settled, talk directly. You need to watch the body language as well as hear the words.

4. *Keep repeating your positive message.* Be professional and generous, giving your rival the recognition he so desperately craves. Offer a way out by suggesting his was a misinterpretation. Elevate the discussion by asking the muckraker probing questions. That lets you shift the focus from you two individuals to the issues.

5. *Play with the idea of joining forces.* Put your anger aside to think of ways George could advance. He'd do anything if convinced it would help his career. Suggest an idea that would require your joint talents.

6. *Report dirty tricks.* If your rival's antics will truly damage your career, expose this immediately to your boss. Document occurrences. Without accusing anyone, ask for a new system or procedure to correct a bad situation.

Solomon Says:

Three ways to overcome the hostility of rivals:

1. Widen your focus. Think beyond your job to what your unit and company need.

2. Volunteer to help your rival. Offer technique tips, share decisions, go the extra mile.

3. Be a team player. It not only can win over rivals, it can boost your own career.

THE SCRIPT

YOU.   George, is the rumor true that you're telling everyone I'm butchering the project?

GEORGE.   Where'd you get an idea like that?

YOU.   I hope what I heard is wrong and maybe we've both misinterpreted. We may not be friends, but we needn't be enemies. Your analytical talent is such an important asset to the work. Tell me specifically where you feel we may be off-track.

GEORGE.   Oh, I think we're moving along pretty well.

YOU.   You know, George, making a success of this project

will highlight your talent and mark you as a rising star in the company.

YOU.   [*reacting to another of George's dirty tricks to make you appear incompetent*]. Boss, I'm not receiving the data I need in time for scheduled discussions. [*George conveniently forgot to send them to you.*] We have to make some changes in the routing of information. Perhaps I could take over the distribution. . .?

GUIDELINE

Mudslinging backfires—allowing muckrakers themselves to become the target.

Their obnoxious behavior reflects poorly on themselves. This prompts decent people to turn against the malicious mudslingers and support their victims instead.

17. Stop Stealing from Me!

Reclaiming ideas or turf from thieving colleagues

Rather than attacks, competition may appear in another form—theft.

You've run up against a brainnapper. Jill exploits your concepts and seizes your ideas to use to her own advantage. As long as she gets what she needs, it doesn't matter how. Last week she actually stole your outline, which she claimed was hers.

She's so used to lying, she can't tell the difference between a fib and a fact. The basic problem is Jill's incompetence. She's out of her league, and even in her own she makes mistakes. She also usurps authority, stretching her assignments to overlap yours. In areas where you're in charge, she'll oppose your decisions by contacting others involved and undercutting you.

Your group is working on a team project where, until lately, individual efforts were recognized. They were until Jill started snatching ideas and claiming credit.

The danger to you is that stealing the credit you're due could very well affect your advancement. But you can't expose Jill without proof.

THE GOAL

Intercept the theft of your ideas.

THE PLAN

1. *Make friends with the grandstander.* Allow her to feel important in areas where she's competent so that she'll have less need to resort to deceit. Drown her with attention and seek her opinions. Offer to work with her to improve the project and her performance. Utilize her as a resource person where she works away from you and the other team members.

2. *Commit your ideas to writing.* When you come up with a good idea prior to the meeting, write it up in a brief memo, date it, and distribute it. Offer to be the note taker at the team meeting. Log the ideas being generated and their sources. Give every member a copy.

3. *Wait to speak.* Be the last, rather than among the first, to offer new ideas not previously discussed. At best, she'll only be able to piggyback an addition to your contribution.

4. *Correct a poor system.* You don't have the power to fire your coworkers, but you still have to produce even when they screw up. If things don't improve, don't whine. Ask your boss for a better breakdown of areas of authority and responsibility.

Solomon Says:

Do's and don'ts to stop highjacking:

DON'T tempt thieves by leaving your ideas or items out in the open for them to grab.

DO take precautions, such as distributing signed copies of your work.

DO imply to crooks, pleasantly, that you're on to what they're doing and you're changing the rules of the game.

THE SCRIPT

YOU. Jill, you're good at computations [*an honest compliment*]. What do you think we can do to decrease the time it takes to. . .

YOU. Jill, we all have some blank areas in our education. I realize your training didn't include this kind of analysis, so let me show you an easy way to. . .

YOU. Boss, as you know, we're not moving along as quickly as you hoped we would. Perhaps changing the procedures would let us be more responsive to your needs.

GUIDELINE
Win over the thief while instituting other relief.

18. I Don't Want Any Part of Your Misconduct

When a coworker presses you to do something wrong

While some colleagues try to steal your ideas, others try to rob you of your integrity.

Oh, oh, that warning bell goes off in your brain. You've run into an exploiter who tries to maneuver you into doing things you have qualms about. You know you should heed the warning and resist the threats, but you're terrified of this underhanded, unethical, contemptible person.

Last month Tammy wanted you to do part of her work. You slipped out of that noose by suggesting she ask the boss for extra time on that task. Today she's coercing you to cover for her while she slips out to meet her boyfriend for a few hours.

Tammy's threat is barely veiled. She's implying that either you do what she wants or she'll hurt and embarrass you. There's not much wiggle room between the rock and the hard place. Now you're beginning to panic, worrying what punishment this intimidator can cause.

THE GOAL

Help the offender do the right thing.

THE PLAN

1. *Buy time.* If you're caught by surprise, you don't need to respond instantly. Try to dismiss the despicable request as if it were a preposterous joke.

2. *Articulate your anger constructively.* If your threatener is persistent, tell her carefully and calmly why you can't comply.

3. *Explain the action you propose.* Get the offender to act properly by offering ways to achieve the same end through legitimate means.

4. *Don't wrestle the alligator—drain the swamp.* If this assistance is

refused and the threat is repeated, invite her to accompany you *right now* to the boss's office.

THE SCRIPT

TAMMY.　All you have to do is say I'm at a meeting with a potential client.

YOU.　　[*laughing*]. I'm glad you're not really serious.

TAMMY.　Oh, but I am. Think about it. This is something you will want to do for me.

YOU.　　Tammy, perhaps there's a better way to get what you want. Why not talk to the boss requesting a few hours of personal leave time?

TAMMY.　I'm not going to admit to him that I have a personal problem.

YOU.　　That sure beats lying, and do you realize that you're asking me to break the rules, too? You know I can't do that.

TAMMY.　Sure you can. Look, I'm going to do this one way or another. If I get caught, I'll report that you helped me.

YOU.　　You'd accuse me of a wrong I didn't commit! If you are my friend, why would you want to get me in trouble? C'mon, we're going in right now to see the boss. I can't let this go. We'll see which one he believes.

GUIDELINE

Bullies with real power wouldn't be desperate for you to do their dirty deeds.

Stand up to threats and pressuring. They don't have the clout you think they have.

19. Your Jokes Aren't Funny—
They're Digs

*How to look good after jokers
lampoon your achievement*

Next we have the coworkers who try to rob you of the enjoyment you deserve from the recognition you've earned.

You just set a record for completing your study on time and on budget. Instead of deserved accolades, however, some of your colleagues are making your important accomplishment seem inconsequential. They make sure others hear their comments.

Larry's jokes are particularly biting. You wonder what charm school he graduated from. You suspect he blasts your achievements to enjoy the attention it brings him. Or maybe he's jealous of you, envious of your opportunity to succeed. Perhaps he's harboring hidden hostility and is out for revenge. Who knows his motives!

Others in the group are laughing, but they're visibly uncomfortable. You don't want to look like a poor sport who can't take a joke, so you laugh, too. But it really hurts.

THE GOAL

Enjoy the recognition you've earned.

THE PLAN

1. *Find your backbone.* Stop laughing at mean-spirited criticism. Without attacking your nasty jokers, firmly, strongly, but politely state why your accomplishment was important to the organization. Your smile should say, "I know what you're doing, but I'm not buying it."

2. *Ask what they might have done differently.* This will expose the jokes for what they actually are—blatant criticism—and reduce future attacks. Also, acknowledge these colleagues as important players, which should help lessen the envy.

3. *Stay issue-oriented.* By seeming to ask advice, you might possibly convert your critics. It's important they understand that their value remains the same. It isn't diminished because yours was enhanced. Also, if what you do affects their work, they want a chance to talk about your decisions.

Solomon Says:

To stand up to clever, demeaning jokers:

- Practice at home. Use a tape recorder to hear how you'll come across. If a friend can videotape you, even better.
- Anticipate the confrontation. Visualize the exchange along with the body language you'll be using.

THE SCRIPT

LARRY. Is it true they're going to engrave your name on a plaque for the president's office? Ha, ha, ha.

YOU. Go ahead and laugh, Larry, but this work is meaningful.

LARRY. Really? What's all the fuss about a little study that few people are going to read?

YOU. Well, that's your opinion and you're entitled to it. I know I did a great job. However, the important thing is that this study will bring the company the kind of publicity that generates new accounts.

YOU. [*confronting Larry in private*]. I don't appreciate your undermining my efforts in front of the group. If you have any problem with the way I handle things, we can talk about it alone without your condescending remarks.

YOU. [*to the group*]. Now tell me, I'd really like to know how you think we can improve on this kind of effort in the future. I'll be glad to credit your ideas with the list of recommendations I'm preparing.

GUIDELINE

If you stand up for yourself, the glory-robbers' derisive humor won't steal your thunder.

20. Cease and Desist with the Disses

*Using humor when boorish
clods enjoy ridiculing you*

Other colleagues disguise their negative or hostile feelings as a joke. But there's nothing to laugh at.

You've always felt sensitive because your nose is a little large. Not as bad as Cyrano's, mind you, but somewhat out of proportion. And you think your ears stick out.

Having been hurt yourself, it particularly bothers you when colleagues delight in making others writhe. Sitting around the lunch table, they are free with put-downs, and some toss racial and ethnic slurs. Their victims, also, are too intimidated to fight back.

You thought when you got out of school and started working, the teasing would stop. But the taunters have found you again. Everything about an office today is more informal. You feel the increased familiarity has led to a cruder and ruder workplace. And you have no idea how to get people to behave with common courtesy.

THE GOAL

Put a stop to the taunting.

THE PLAN

1. *Expose nasty remarks for what they are.* Really mean remarks are disguised hostility. Angry jokes hurt and aren't funny, even happening to somebody else. First try a nonconfrontational approach rather than a verbal punch. While you should feel enraged, you don't want to give the clods a legitimate grievance against you. Keep notes (dates, witnesses, conversations) that you'll use later if you are unable to sensitize the offenders.

2. *Toss mocking comments right back.* While there's a serious difference between teasing banter and hostile attacks, in both cases at least appear to lighten up. Act self-assured as you respond to your tormentor.

3. *Kid the kidder*. Rehearse a few retorts. Go the teaser one better. Carry the joke one step further. If you refuse to get mad or flustered, you take away the fun of teasing you. So learn how to poke fun at yourself.

Solomon Says:

When teasers step over the line, try:

- Delivering a verbal hotfoot. Warn them—for their own sakes—that being too cute will backfire not only in the workplace but also at home and among friends.

- Stating how their remarks make you feel.

- Staying composed, keeping eye contact, and speaking lower and slower.

THE SCRIPT

LUKE. Can't you people learn how to speak English?

YOU. [*copying the sage's retort*]. You make me so angry, I'm inviting you outside. Please leave.

• • •

LUKE. That's some absurd outfit you have on today!

YOU. It's a good thing nobody put you in charge of the dress code.

• • •

LUKE. What kind of report is that? Did your son help you put it together?

YOU. [*your best imitation of Ronald Reagan*]. There you go again. . .trying to humiliate me. . . Can't you criticize professionally? It's really clever the way you make a fool of yourself.

• • •

LUKE. All I said was that you took a heck of a long time to turn in the data. Why are you so defensive? It's a joke.

YOU. Why do you think I'm being defensive? I just don't understand your comment. Explain it to me. You know, Luke, we all can't be as magnificently expert as you in screwing up.

• • •

LUKE. You know, your ears are so large that—

YOU. [*interrupting*]. Absolutely. But maybe you don't know I'm blessed with remarkable powers. My ears are so large that I hear what's going on all over the office. Ha, ha.

GUIDELINE
Self-deprecating humor leaves no room for ridicule.

21. We Can Salvage This

*When partnerships are threatened
by intense disagreements*

Going into business with a friend requires extreme caution.

Ever since college, Chris and Dottie have been good friends. Two years ago it seemed like a great idea for them to open an office together as equal partners. Both were skilled in the field of child care and saw the need for consultants to work with businesses desiring to establish child care centers. Their concept was paying off as their list of clients grew steadily.

But now they realize being friends isn't enough for a business/professional relationship to survive. Their differences in personalities and approaches to problem-solving are causing daily disruptions.

Chris sees the big picture. She can get carried away and admits to making major decisions without consulting her partner, contrary to what they both agreed to originally. Dottie is more task oriented. She's precise and critical and admits she may inflict pain with her frankness.

They have virtually stopped talking to each other, communicating through Don, their office manager. This scene is much like parents who argue and use a child to deliver messages back and forth, a practice that has only widened the gap. So now they're at a crossroads. The office is suffering and can't survive many more heated arguments. Both, however, are willing to give it another try.

THE GOAL

Keep the partnership intact.

THE PLAN

1. *Talk directly to each other*. Stop going through a third party. Messages can get misinterpreted. Remember the kids' game of telephone? By the time the last person revealed the communication it was unrecognizable.

2. *Examine activities each finds helpful and hurtful*. Meet outside the office in neutral territory. Set ground rules for your frank discussion. For example, it's been proven effective for one to speak for a few minutes—uninterrupted—while the other listens. The other person has to paraphrase what was said and then has equal time. The idea is to concentrate on the message and not on one's response or defense. Arrange a signal when the language or body language becomes inflammatory. Hopefully, the talk will include what brought you together in the first place.

3. *Set up safeguards.* Invest in good legal and accounting advice. Get help in establishing a solid structure of accountability and controls and ways to avoid deadlock when both partners can't agree.

THE SCRIPT

CHRIS. I think our biggest problem is the different views about where we want to go from here. Now's the time to expand, even if it means putting in more capital. You are so project oriented that you want to wait until every *t* is crossed and these golden opportunities pass us by.

DOTTIE. You're right when you say I want to wait to expand. These opportunities may or may not be good. We won't know until we give it careful study. We can't afford to go off half-cocked.

CHRIS. Well, obviously, we can't decide by ourselves the best way to proceed. I'm agreeable to hiring good counselors. First we need someone who doesn't know either of us so they can be independent in helping us heal the rift in our relationship.

DOTTIE. That's a good first step. But we also need expert advice from a CPA and an attorney who deals in partnership agreements. It's clear to me that we should have spelled out a lot of things before we ever started, like setting up controls and handling disputes.

CHRIS. Praise the Lord, we finally agree about something.

GUIDELINE
Friendship alone won't assure a successful partnership.

Consider how personality differences affect operations and use outside advice to set up controls.

Chapter IV

Clients and Customers

When you are giving a service or providing a product, every client and customer counts. You try to make each one feel special. You're in business and if you don't connect by satisfying the client or making the sale, it's a safe bet your competitor will.

So you bend over backwards trying to please people who are impossible. Some are so used to instant gratification, they demand special and unreasonable attention. Management today is beginning to delegate decision-making to lower levels. These people are being trained to meet customer as well as supervisory needs on the spot.

There are also clients who bother you at home with phone calls at ungodly hours. Not getting exactly what they want, they can become abusive. Others lie to you or fail to give you the whole story, which makes helping them that much more difficult.

Somehow you must link up with these exasperating customers and clients to establish a mutually satisfactory relationship. Although you can't always oblige them, you have to speak obligingly to ensure your continuing income from them.

22. I Appreciate Your Business, But...

Handling impatient egotists demanding special treatment

Some people believe paying for a service entitles them to be as obnoxious as they want to be.

Mrs. Black is a bully in a designer suit. Being subtle with her doesn't work. She issues orders that require giving her extra attention at the expense of other clients. Her time, she feels, is more important.

In a haughty manner, Mrs. Black is a dehumanizer, treating people like objects. She thinks paying your agency a hefty sum allows her to be rude to you and your staff. It's particularly troublesome when other clients are within earshot of her loud, disruptive voice.

Not to create a scene, you've been giving in while she oversteps the rules of civility and stomps on everyone's toes. She would have you reorganize your whole office to suit her preferences. It's all you can do to control your temper. You're wondering if it's worth trying to win her over.

THE GOAL
Snatch the impetus back from the bully.

You can't change Mrs. Black, but you can change the way you react to her commands.

THE PLAN
1. *Stop kowtowing.* You provide a service, but this is also a business. You have to take care of your legitimate needs or you won't remain in business. If you don't take a stand, you lose everyone's respect—Mrs. Black's, your other clients, your staff, and your own.

2. *Start with the client's legitimate interests.* Extract from her exactly what she feels she needs from you, for example, whom to contact if there's a problem. Listen closely because an outspoken client sometimes says what less talkative unhappy clients are thinking.

3. *Calmly and briefly explain your position.* Tell why you need to adhere to your policies. Even if you risk losing her account, you save the other ones and build your business on a solid footing. Don't pay attention if she tags you with undesirable adjectives. Avoid any critical frontal jabs. Your polite, firm resolve to no longer tolerate her abusive behavior is a sufficient counterpunch. Express your appreciation for past business and your promise to keep her informed, but maintain that you must stick to your rules.

4. *Clarify your mutual interests.* When clients understand that you have to do certain things in a particular way in order to take care of their needs, it dawns on them that you're in this together for joint benefit. Show her how to get what she wants from future business with you.

THE SCRIPT

YOU.   Mrs. Black, spell it out for me. I want to be sure I understand what it is that you need and expect from my agency.

MRS. B. I have to have prompt delivery. That's essential. Sometimes there have been delays. I need to move quickly and not be kept waiting all the time. Your agency has to shape up and deal with these inefficiencies.

YOU.   I understand your concerns.

MRS. B. And I don't see why you ask me for a deposit with my orders. You know I am good for the money.

YOU.   Of course. And we appreciate your business, Mrs. Black. But don't take the request personally. As you can see from this book of photocopied deposit checks given us by other clients, this is standard practice that we must adhere to. These are policies that allow us to provide maximum services to you and our other clients at a reduced rate. Now let me tell you what we can do, by working together, to speed up the delivery. From now on. . .

GUIDELINE
Showing your sincere interest will dam a flood of fiats.

23. Let's Discuss This in Private

Calming angry folks who are using loud and abusive language

Please and appease—that's one of the first rules drummed into sales-people along with The Customer Is Always Right. But a company's stand-there-and-take-it policy takes a tremendous toll on employees who are targets of verbal abuse.

You work in a large, exclusive clothing store whose policy puts you right in the middle. You feel you have a right to be treated with the basic civility due every person.

Today a customer was in a fury over the delay when he came to pick up the suit he had bought and left to be altered. You tried to explain what had happened, but he must have misunderstood you. He threw a tantrum, and his threats kept getting louder and louder.

You couldn't quiet his insulting screams. It was a very embarrassing experience taking place in front of many other customers. So you called the manager, who then led the man away to talk to him in the privacy of his office.

You know you do as good a job as most employees, and probably better. But right now you feel as if you've been punched in the stomach by a bully. What can you do in the future to stop such a verbal barrage?

THE GOAL

Balance protecting your position without losing the customer.

THE PLAN

1. *Stop, look, and listen.* A person who's upset can't process your explanation. Whatever your reason, it sounds like an alibi to him. So stop spouting logic or screaming back. Look directly at the ranter, and without interrupting listen carefully to what's being said. If you're not alone facing this kind of problem, suggest that management might offer a training session on how to de-escalate arguments.

2. *View complaints as opportunities to improve service.* You cannot take tantrums personally—it's the customer who's having the problem. However, this does give you the chance to conduct your own grassroots research without the aid of expensive marketing tools. What you hear can be refined and filtered to fit your organization. You can help resolve issues important to the customer.

3. *Let your customers be heard.* What they want more than anything else is for you to listen and really hear what they're saying. Let the customers know you realize they're upset, annoyed, or inconvenienced without judging their behavior. If you insensitively and instantly reject the complaint (that's the way your explanation would be perceived), the resentment is much more difficult to overcome.

4. *Get right to the solution.* Summarize the issue factually, impersonally. Show a willingness to compromise, if necessary. Ask dissatisfied customers what they're after and how they want you to handle the matter, letting them join in the problem solving. Usually this is simpler, cheaper, and faster than you would have imagined. And it keeps him from telling a couple of dozen friends not to patronize you. It's vital to keep a customer from going elsewhere. Some studies show it costs five times as much to recruit a new customer as it does to retain an old one.

5. *Make sure your apology is sincere.* Don't add fuel to the fire with an insulting apology, qualifying it with "*if* I offended you." Reasonable or not, the customer was offended. Emphasize your sincerity by acknowledging the other's feelings, calling the customer by name and being careful not to attack his point of view.

THE SCRIPT

You. Mr. Dickson, according to the ticket, your suit was promised for five o'clock. I'm sorry but it's only three and it hasn't come down yet. Perhaps you could—

Him. I've been coming here for years and this is no way to treat a good customer. You call alterations and have them bring that suit down immediately.

You. I did call and—

HIM.   Don't you be insolent with me or I'll have your job. If my suit is not being worked on right now, I'm canceling my order and you'll never see me in this store again.

YOU.   [*lowering your voice*]. Mr. Dickson, I'm truly sorry that what I said offended you. Thank you for explaining your position. I understand that it would be a great inconvenience for you to wait two hours or to have to make another trip here. Tell me what you would like me to do about this.

HIM.   Well, first advise the tailor that you have a good customer down here waiting for his suit and determine how much more time he needs to finish the alteration. Since no one else is waiting, if he's not working on my suit right now, tell him to drop everything else and do so.

YOU.   That's an excellent suggestion. I'll do that immediately.

GUIDELINE

Ranting stops when others believe you're truly listening to what they have to say.

Acknowledge the customers' feelings and ask clarifying questions in order to agree on the real problem before you discuss solutions.

24. Quit Bullying Me

Stopping unwarranted pestering at home and in the office

While much attention is directed at keeping the clients you have, let's look at the other side of the coin. Some people you cater to are rude, disruptive, demanding, and arrogant.

Presently you have a couple of pushy clients who are driving you crazy. They are obsessive and clinging. They call your home in the middle of the night. They barge into your office without an appointment whenever they have a new complaint and are so agitated they can't wait to air it.

Because they feel abused, they expect the whole world to drop everything at any time to seek remedial action for them. You find yourself a victim of these avengers determined to right a wrong.

You've tried reasoning with them and they agree to respect normal business hours and office courtesy. Then something happens to upset them and they're waking up your whole family with telephone calls. What can you do?

THE GOAL
Reinstate yourself as controller of your business and your life.

THE PLAN
1. *Recognize bullies who masquerade as clients.* They intimidate you by throwing their weight around. You don't want to lose the account, but when you allow them to get away with this behavior, they regard you as weak. Only when you stand up for yourself do they admire your strength. Remove the weight from your shoulders by changing your response.

2. *Lay down the law.* You can be friendly and forceful simultaneously as you fight back to hold your own. Calmly and unemotionally, state your position. Do this without directly criticizing the clients.

3. *Be willing to let these people go.* The price you've been paying for their revenue is too high. You've been selling your soul at the cost of respect—theirs and yours. You have to be in control of your office and able to protect the privacy of your home. If they refuse to play by your rules, send them away. Chances are once you are clear and firm, they will abide. If not, you'll no longer be drained by their demands and can concentrate on replacing them.

Solomon Says:

To control bullying:

- DO lift that boulder from your shoulder. Realize that imposers weigh you down by interrupting and pulverizing your time schedule.
- DON'T let them call the shots—you lose more than you gain if you continue to do so.

THE SCRIPT

CLIENT. [2:05 A.M.]. I'm sorry to call you so late, but I just thought of something great you could use in my case and. . .

YOU. You woke me up at two o'clock in the morning when it's not an emergency? What's the matter with you?

CLIENT. This is important and you promised to go all out to help me.

YOU. Yes, I did. I want you to be in my office at 9:30 sharp and we will discuss this.

• • •

YOU. [9:30 A.M.]. If you ever call me again at home, no matter the hour, our relationship is through. I do not conduct business at home. Clients come to the office by appointment only. That's the way it has to be. I am glad for you

to continue as my client if you can accept my office procedures. If you can't, you will have to find someone else
to take your case.

GUIDELINE

Run your office your way—don't let intrusive clients push you around.
Demanding clients have no respect for you when you let them
intimidate you. Worse yet, you lose your self-respect unless you stand
up to them.

25. It's Time to Fish or Cut Bait

*When their vacillating
stops the sale*

Customers who keep flip-flopping are exasperating.

You're feeling very frustrated and angry after dealing with Mr. Dalton. A good sale is slipping away because of his indecisiveness. You left him agreeing to the purchase only to have him call back a few hours later saying he wanted to wait awhile.

So you persuaded him again. Again, he wavered. No amount of coaxing or cajoling can get him to commit. What works with your other customers doesn't work with Dalton.

This pleasant fellow seems to want to please you or, at least, not to hurt your feelings. Perhaps he's thinking that if he stalls long enough, the need for a decision will disappear along with the opportunity.

In the meantime, this wishy-washy behavior has sapped your energy and enthusiasm. You've explained all the benefits ad nauseam. How else can you nudge him to act?

THE GOAL
Convince the customer to make a decision and stick to it.

THE PLAN
1. *Dig for the reasons behind the stall.* Something is keeping the vacillator from going ahead. He himself may not be aware of the reason. Tone down your own enthusiasm to free the indecisive one from feeling guilty about hurting you if he doesn't proceed.

2. *Suggest alternatives.* If you overwhelmed him with information, simplify the options and consequences. Together look at the facts and logical answers to the problems your probing has uncovered.

3. *Reassure him he's doing the right thing.* Support his decision by following up to prevent a relapse. When you call back to see if he's still gung-ho, you can clear up any reservations.

Three ways to get the wishy-washy to decide:

1. Simplify your language, translating technical terms into English.

2. Get the customer to tell you the hang-up and the results hoped for.

3. Narrow the choices, giving guidelines to point up what's most important to the buyer.

THE SCRIPT

YOU. [*gently probing*]. Mr. Dalton, I know even the very best products have certain aspects that could pose a problem for customers. I'd really appreciate your telling me what you think should be altered.

DALTON. [*not wanting to offend you*]. Well, I think the overall quality is rather good.

YOU. [*picking up on the qualifying words*]. Rather good? What would make it very good? Is there something about the construction? Do you think it's strong enough to meet your purpose? Perhaps if you see a higher grade, you could then choose what's best for you.

• • •

YOU. [*follow up*]. Mr. Dalton, I'm just checking to see that we've cleared up any questions you might have. . .I really think you've made a good choice. . .I can stop by Monday or Wednesday to finalize the order [*minor decision technique*]. Which day is better for you?

GUIDELINE
Move indecisives—unearth the real reason behind the stall.

26. I Made a Mistake; Can We Start Over?

Making amends after you step on someone's sensibilities

It's you who must pay the price when customers feel you've degraded them.

You've been suspended without pay pending a company investigation for just stating your feelings. As the manager of a chain bakery, you refused to write Happy Birthday in Spanish on a cake for the woman's aged father. When she offered to write out the greeting for the frosting, you again rebuffed her with the comment, "This is America and we only write in English."

Having lived in the United States for three decades, the shocked and angry customer complained to the company. Officials assured her it was their policy to fulfill requests for Spanish-language writing on cakes in all their stores.

Hit with the suspension, you admitted the stupidity of your comments and apologized for embarrassing your company. Now you're sweating out losing your job.

THE GOAL

Survive the crisis and regain the confidence of officials.

THE PLAN

1. *Accept full responsibility*. You made a mistake, now express a desire to make amends. Point out your good record up until now. Ask for another chance to prove yourself an asset to the organization.

2. *Assure investigators you'll promote company policy*. Tell them you're not only willing to accept company policy, but you'll also further it, without pay, on your own time. If allowed to continue, it'll take quite a while to reestablish trust.

3. *Offer to demonstrate your sincerity*. Whether or not the company accepts your proposal is not as important as showing you understand that unless a company policy is illegal or immoral, all workers must adhere. Showing yourself as an idea person may put you back in the plus column.

Solomon Says:

Two keys to controlling your panic:

1. When you first realize the potential consequences of your blunder, remind yourself that we all make mistakes. Stop everything for a minute of deep breathing.

2. Plan your acknowledgment. Saying you're sorry isn't sufficient. The apology needs to be soon enough, sincere enough, and strong enough to abate anger.

THE SCRIPT

YOU. I am truly sorry that my rash and offensive comments to a customer embarrassed the company. I realize now how wrong it was and how my action could have hurt business. To make up for my lapse of judgment and to show my loyalty to the company, I'd like to suggest a way to erase this unpleasantness while making new friends for us. I propose that we offer a public service with my conducting a class in cake writing and, of course, alerting the Latino areas that the program will be bilingual.

GUIDELINE

Put meat on the bones of your apology.

Don't just give lip service saying you're sorry someone took your remark the wrong way. Show you understand why your action was wrong and you'll put forth time and energy to make it right.

27. This Accusation Doesn't Have Merit

When unfounded attacks can ruin reputations or get you fired

In your medical office you've been following rules set down by Fran, the former office manager. When Josie recently replaced Fran, she made no effort to alter the policy of collecting fees from patients in advance of the visits.

Today a patient, affronted by your request for payment, complained to Josie. The customer said you were impudent and demanding of someone who always paid his bills on time. You thought you were being firm and courteous.

The new manager attempted to appease the patient by blaming you for an unauthorized offense. Everybody within earshot heard her say, "She'll apologize to you or her job is in jeopardy." Startled and humiliated, instead of saying you were sorry about the offense, you began to explain that you were only following established policy. Expecting an apology, the patient became more enraged and Josie evidently felt betrayed.

The rest of the staff watched, mentally taking sides, as the atmosphere became increasingly tense. It won't help you get another job if you're fired from this one. You still don't think it was your fault. You went by the rules and the patient misinterpreted your request.

THE GOAL

To keep your job.

THE PLAN

1. *Say nothing for now.* Sure you're justified in feeling angry about criticism you feel was unwarranted. You don't have to forget it, just control blowing up. Remind yourself that you risk your job by telling off your supervisor or rallying support against her.

2. *Try to understand the behavior.* Listen intently to figure out what brought on the warning. No one condones yellow-bellied action—yes, Josie should have taken responsibility for the policy and made an exception with this patient, if she wished. However, you may hear that the manager, being new, is scared and desperate to keep her own job.

3. *Sound understanding.* Meet with your boss. No excuse, no apology, just show you can tell she's upset. Obviously, she's in no mood to hear what would sound like an alibi to her. And telling her she's wrong and should share a good part of the blame won't raise your stock either.

4. *Present a reality check.* After she winds down, recite the bare facts, free of blame or emotion. Together examine what could have prevented the conflict. Shift gears to resolving the matter. Making helpful suggestions for her consideration may peg you as someone worth keeping around.

THE SCRIPT

JOSIE. Tony, we're not going to have any patients left the way you've gone around insulting everyone.

YOU. [*not answering the charge*]. Josie, you say the patient was offended and I'm truly sorry that gave you trouble.

JOSIE. We simply can't afford another incident like that.

YOU. You're right. [*Move right to the issue, away from your actions.*] Fran established a policy that's not working out the way she anticipated. Now that you're the manager, you'll probably want to make changes to avoid future misunderstandings.

JOSIE. Yes, we need to be clear about how to request payment without offending the patients.

YOU. Have you considered posting a tactful sign in the reception area? We could express our appreciation to our patients for their understanding of our payment policy and if there's a problem to please talk to us about it.

GUIDELINE:
Hold your fire and your excuses.

Perceived as alibis, excuses inflame the finger pointers. By offering positive solutions, you also concentrate on your own objective.

Chapter V

Doctors, Lawyers, and Other Professional Experts

Doctors, lawyers, accountants—whatever the profession, the people in them are simply human beings. Although their attitudes often send another message, they are no more important than you. They are just individuals highly trained to give advice or service for which you pay highly.

If you elevate professionals to the status of gods, you can't expect them to treat you as their equal. Like everyone else, they deserve your respect and courtesy. But they are not omnipotent.

So if they make you miserable because they seem haughty, arrogant, high-handed, inattentive, or insensitive, *you* might be sending out wrong signals.

28. Do You Understand What I Want?

*Getting the high and mighty to
pay attention to what you're saying*

You're well satisfied with the care your medical doctor gives you, but you find the starched coat hard to talk to. When you try to explain a problem, you get the feeling he doesn't hear what you're saying. Or you're taking up too much of his valuable time.

Maybe you're boring him because he's way ahead of you. Maybe your comments are insignificant. Whatever it is, you have an uneasy sensation.

He prides himself on keeping to his schedule. So if you come in because of a sore throat, he seems to resent your asking him how to treat the backaches you've been having lately. It's like, "That isn't on the menu for today."

Instead of feeling good after a visit, you feel mad at yourself for not being a better communicator. What can you say to the doctor to keep his attention?

THE GOAL
Have your concerns acknowledged.

THE PLAN
1. *Decide to speak up.* Give yourself a much needed pep talk. After all, you are as important an individual as your doctor, lawyer, accountant, or any other professional. They get paid, usually quite well, for being highly trained, but you are the one paying for their services. You'll always be afraid to confront until you take the plunge and dive in.

2. *Plan your conversation.* Be honest about your feelings. Chances are the doctor has no idea you feel this way. Although the medical profession is a high calling, it's still a business and doctors are very upset when patients choose not to continue coming to them.

3. *Ask how communication attempts can be more significant.* Discuss the manner in which he likes patients to reveal a problem.

Solomon Says:

When professionals are unresponsive:

- DON'T take the pomposity personally. Each of their patients or clients is treated to the same arrogance.
- DO ask for better treatment or switch to another provider if you feel offended. You owe this to yourself.

THE SCRIPT

YOU. Dr. Forth, I'm feeling a little troubled about the way we are communicating. I get the feeling that I may be presenting information that is insignificant. [*You're tactfully confronting without accusing.*]

DR.. No, no, I want you to tell me whatever is on your mind.

YOU. But you don't seem to be hearing what I say.

DR.. Oh, I hear you all right. I'm just relating in my mind what you are saying to your overall condition.

YOU. Maybe it would be helpful to both of us if you'd tell me what specific information you need. Would you like me to come in with a written record of some kind?

DR.. OK, the first thing we need to know is. ...

GUIDELINE

Don't assume you know what another is thinking.

If you feel upset or ignored, confront by tactfully asking for clarification.

29. Your Arrogance Is Discomforting to Me

*When replies to your queries
make you feel stupid*

Other professionals hear you quite well but respond in an arrogant manner.

You went to the attorney because you needed help. You were feeling vulnerable and defeated, and your spirit was punctured. The last thing you needed was to be treated like a child who couldn't possibly understand what's going on.

But you knew you were in the office of a very busy lawyer and this made you even more nervous. Mr. Dennis Knowles let you know he's an authority in the field and his time is valuable.

Humbled before such a legal giant, you carefully and politely phrased your questions. And you felt miserable when you were told, in effect, that you didn't need to know the answers and couldn't comprehend them if you did.

You need this lawyer's skill and help; you don't need his derision and disdain. How can you overcome his patronizing attitude and reach a better relationship?

THE GOAL
Extract the information you deserve to have.

THE PLAN
1. *Straighten your spine and stop groveling.* You've been letting him walk all over you. Assuming you're up to date on your bill, you have paid for a service. It's time to establish equal footing. If Mr. Knowles calls you by your first name, return the favor and call him Dennis. Smile as though you're glad you came. Stand and sit tall to project the self-confidence you may not be feeling. Body language is the first step in commanding respect. Look him directly in the eye as you speak slowly and firmly.

2. *Know your rights.* When the state licenses lawyers, it insists that lawyers keep clients fully informed or risk disbarment.

3. *Object to any put-down with a smile or joke.* Fling it right back. These people are tough, they can take it. Only by standing up to them will you gain their respect.

4. *State your questions succinctly.* Unless pain and suffering is the issue, don't preface your queries with emotional talk. You're after the facts. You want to know how ABC affects XYZ.

Solomon Says:

Three strategies for handling condescenders:

1. Earn their respect. Concisely and precisely state what concerns you. Skip the preamble. Quantify when possible— this type likes to deal in numbers.

2. Prepare questions in advance. Solid ones ("How does this compare to…?" "What other factors influence…?")

3. Challenge them to tell you what you want. Bright, quick, impatient people can't resist showing off how fast they can react.

THE SCRIPT

YOU.   [*previously subservient*]. Mr. Knowles, may I ask you [*what made you think you needed permission?*] about the progress of my case? What is the effect of this new motion?

KNOWLES.   Oh, Helen, it's too technical and complicated to explain. But trust me. By filing this motion, we're taking care of the problem in the best way.

• • •

YOU.   [*new approach*]. Good morning, Dennis. How is my case coming along? I'd like to hear a progress report.

KNOWLES.   Lovely lady, don't you worry your head about that.

YOU.   Lovely man, [*smiling but assertive*] I do worry and I
           need an explanation. And you'll find me most
           capable of comprehending. Now, at what stage are
           we at this time, and exactly what's left to be
           decided?

GUIDELINE
Professionals are just people—don't treat them as gods.

Insist on getting what you pay for. You can be firm yet cordial. This is simply exchanging brain power for a fee.

30. In Plain English, Please

*When they speak in terms
lay people can't comprehend*

You need hip boots to make your way through their incomprehensible muck.

You're a paralegal at a law firm where each attorney has an ego more massive than the next. You ask a question and the response is pedantic. They always give you much more information than you need to do your work.

Choosing to impress with legal terminology, likewise, has clients struggling to grasp the meaning. One can plainly see the puzzled looks. Replies are often pompous, filled with longer words when shorter ones would be better. You suspect, at times, they toss out technical terms to avoid admitting they have to look up a certain point.

Maybe they think their gibberish elevates them in the eyes of people not in their profession. But as far as you're concerned, the manipulative and ambiguous double-talk is driving you wild.

You really would like to tell them how you and others react to the jargon, both for your sake and for that of the firm. And how can you get them to tell you just the essentials?

THE GOAL
Clear up the murky gobbledygook.

THE PLAN
1. *Gently alert your bosses.* Tactfully say that you've observed that their clients need more down-to-earth explanations. They should infer that you say this because you want to help the firm grow.

2. *Propose they furnish specific facts.* Rather than letting them speak in generalities and unfamiliar, roundabout phrases, encourage them to pin down the numbers involved, give examples, and focus on the main point.

3. *Suggest they translate technical language.* Give an example where plain English would simplify and clarify their message. Afterwards, when they pile on the jargon with you, you can good-naturedly point to another example.

Solomon Says:

To better understand what's going on:

- DON'T accept long, wordy, vague, pompous explanations that go over your head.
- DO insist on language you can understand—you're paying for that information.
- DON'T apologize for failing to comprehend the gibberish. Simply and politely request that it be put in comprehensible terms.

THE SCRIPT

YOU. I see how hard you're working to increase profits for the firm. May I tell you something I've observed that could possibly help?

BOSS. By all means.

YOU. You might want to think about the way you are conveying information to your clients. Some tell me they're confused by the legal terminology. They don't have the background to grasp a lot of what you're saying and seem too timid to ask you to explain, so they stop by my desk and question me. I tell them to talk directly to you.

BOSS. Yes, that's what you should say. You can't be put in the position of giving clients legal advice. What seems to trouble them?

YOU. I'll give you an example: Mr. Hutchin's appeal on his right, as a unit owner, to dock his boat at his condo association's dock. The motion asked the court to vacate its ruling enforcing an injunction against Mr. Hutchin. You told him the trial court abused its discretion in denying the motion to vacate because he did not receive a copy of the order in time to allow an appeal. Mr. Hutchin was confused about "vacate" which he thought meant he had to remove his boat, rather than, I think, you meant the ruling against him would be annulled. Clients don't understand these legal terms. It would help if you translated them into simple English. Also, I'd like to suggest being a little more specific, with examples and descriptions.

GUIDELINE

When smart people are dumb communicators, your tactful criticism will help you and the firm.

31. Love Your Waiting Room, But...

Voicing your complaint about being kept waiting

It may sound like heresy, but some physicians confide that other doctors intentionally overbook, believing there is nothing wrong with keeping patients waiting. You understand that emergencies happen and if you had an emergency, you'd want to be taken out of turn. But when there's a pattern of waiting over an hour every time, something is wrong.

After the receptionist says the doctor will be with you shortly, you sit and wait an hour or two with no explanation. If you're ill, you're too miserable to think straight. But you're there for a routine checkup, and you're frustrated. You have so much to do. You arrived on time, and you're fuming over the imposition. You're ready to tell the receptionist off when your name is finally called.

Then you know the routine. You're ushered into an examining room, instructed to disrobe into a flimsy paper gown. The nurse smiles, saying the doctor will be with you in a minute, knowing full well that one minute can stretch into another thirty.

How can you improve the situation for the future?

THE GOAL
Establish the fact that your time is also valuable.

THE PLAN
1. *Call to confirm the actual time.* Before you leave for the office, ask if the doctor is running late and agree on a new adjusted time for you to come in.

2. *Make any waiting time more meaningful.* Plan ahead with a Things to Do While Waiting List. Bring the paperback or magazine you couldn't get to. A pad for ideas on the talk you have to give.

Stationery and pen to write notes you've been putting off. Even better, concentrate on relaxing. Close your eyes and meditate, oblivious to everyone else in the room.

3. *Express your discontent.* Tell the one who books appointments that you are upset because your time is also valuable. Ask to be informed, honestly, how long it will be because you have other appointments that you must keep. If too long, reschedule and leave.

4. *Discuss this problem with your doctor.* Make sure he or she knows how long you have to wait every time and ask why they can't institute a better system.

THE SCRIPT

YOU. [*to the receptionist*]. I'd like to discuss your booking practice. From what I've observed, you double book patients. We all show up at the same time and then have to sit around and wait for an hour. That's not fair and it's very frustrating.

REC. We have to have a system like that to protect against times that patients don't show.

YOU. OK, but I spend one hour waiting and five minutes with the doctor. My time is valuable, too. Until you come up with a better system, I think it would be reasonable from now on if I call you before I leave for your office. You can adjust the time of my appointment if the doctor is running late. Either that, or reduce the fee for my visit to compensate me for my wasted time.

REC. You've always been punctual. That's a good idea. You call me before you're ready to leave, and I'll tell you when to come in.

YOU. [*to your doctor*]. Doc, I feel I'm getting the right care here, but frankly, I can't afford the long waiting room time. This happens each time I come, so I conclude the delay is not from emergencies.

DOC. Chuck, you know I'm not sitting in my office with my feet propped up. I move as fast as I can. If you needed extra time, I would give it to you.

You. Of course. I applaud both your dedication and your expertise. I'm suggesting that there are new scheduling techniques that might work better and reduce frustration level among captive patients.

Doc. I find it frustrating, too. They didn't teach us business management in med school.

You. In one sense, you and I are both businessmen. We each offer a service. What do you think is a reasonable time for patients to be kept waiting?

Doc. I'd say about fifteen minutes, but if there are emergencies, about a half hour.

You. I agree. I don't think you realize that most of us wait over an hour to see you. So as one businessman to another, don't you agree that whoever's managing your practice should review the scheduling procedure?

Doc. Yes, I do. Your remarks have been an eye opener.

GUIDELINE

Professionals are also business people who don't want their practice put in jeopardy.

So speak up when you have a legitimate complaint. They need to hear and correct poor procedures.

Chapter VI

Salespersons and Service Providers

Most of us feel frustrated, taken, or angry when a purchase or service is not what we expected or paid for. Yet the majority of customers don't complain; we just take our business somewhere else. If we do complain and the experience is unpleasant enough, we'll spread word of mistreatment to another twenty people.

Because it's much cheaper for businesses to retain customers than to find new ones, handling complaints well is an important economic consideration for them. So whether the product is shoddy, the service is rotten, or the employees make it clear they don't give a tinker's damn about your needs, you'll find it worth your while to speak up. Most companies today will take your complaint seriously. They've learned that a customer isn't really a customer until he's a repeat customer. They know the value of consistency in product and service. By voicing what's wrong, you are helping them with market research.

But you do need to know how to complain constructively to the individuals who represent the businesses. And you need to know what recourse you have if that doesn't work.

32. You Sold Me a Bad Bill of Goods

*How to complain about
a product to get results*

Today you're in a tizzy. You found the perfect jacket and after you wore the jacket twice, the zipper broke. You paid a little more to get what you thought was a better toaster-oven. So on the lowest setting, why does it burn your toast every morning? The rug you ordered was supposed to be delivered three months ago and with each day your frustration is mounting. And how about the car you rented that stopped running on your way to the airport?

You know the story, just fill in your own product. If the salesperson is nasty about satisfying your complaint, you'll probably never set foot in that store again. On the other hand, if he or she is obliging, you'll most likely remain loyal.

The problem now is how to express your complaint so that you'll get the results you want.

THE GOAL

Secure an outcome you deem acceptable.

THE PLAN

1. *Decide what you want.* A refund, a credit, a replacement, a repair? Sometimes you just want an apology.

2. *Gather pertinent data.* Find the sales receipt, your canceled check, or credit card statement, any contract, warranty, or relevant printed material. If you make any phone calls on this matter, jot down the date and person to whom you spoke and the gist of the conversation.

3. *Summarize the problem.* Write out in one simple sentence what went wrong. (The toaster burns my toast; the zipper is defective; the rug delivery is not as promised; the car conked out.) Just the facts, keep your anger out of it. Then another sentence stating the result you want.

4. *Contact the store.* Some clerks are empowered to deal with these kinds of problems. If you sense you are not being properly helped, turn to the supervisor, manager, or owner. Don't argue with the clerk. Insist on speaking to the person who is authorized to make decisions. Get the name and position of the speaker and when appropriate action will occur. Send a thank-you note for the help. Call back before the deadline to check progress.

5. *Call the manufacturer.* If you're not satisfied with the answer, check your papers for an 800 telephone number to speak to a customer representative. Most companies realize that they have to satisfy complaints in order to stay competitive.

6. *Write a complaint letter that works.* Address it to the president of the company. Keep your letter businesslike, polite, and to the point. State what's wrong, when and where you purchased it/them, and what you want done. Enclose *copies* (you keep originals) of sales slips and warranties. By indicating a copy is going to the Better Business Bureau, you're saying somebody else is watching. Even if you don't get exactly what you ask for, you'll most likely get a reasonable compromise.

Solomon Says:

When you want to complain:

- DON'T go on and on without coming up for air, or the real problem gets lost in the maze.

- DO immediately identify the issue. It helps to write it down beforehand.

- DON'T whine, scream, or threaten.

- DO be pleasant, controlling your anger. No accusations—you get more with honey, etc.

- DON'T impute a bad motive—nobody's out to get you.

- DO state solutions, such as how you think the matter should be settled or what the procedure should be in the future.

THE SCRIPT

YOU. [*calm, firm, and friendly, explaining the situation to the one who sold you the item*]. There's something wrong with this toaster-oven. Even on the lowest setting, it burns my toast. I would like a refund, please.

CLERK. [*nasty, as though you attacked him personally*]. You must be doing something wrong. You must not have followed directions. We've never had a complaint about this item. What kind of bread are you using?

YOU. What difference does that make? The appliance is defective and I want a refund. Since you can't help me, tell me where I can find the manager.

YOU. [*if friendly and reasonable doesn't work with the manager*]. You leave me no choice but to take other action [*notifying appropriate agencies, consumer protection reporters, and two dozen of your closest friends*].

GUIDELINE

Complain constructively, being clear about what you want.

Even if it's just about aspirin that came crushed, the manufacturer probably will replace it and send you free coupons to keep your business and reward you for your feedback.

33. This Isn't What I Paid For!

*How to complain
when the service isn't as promised*

Lashing out over poor service is a natural reaction. But you've more to gain using your brain.

Henry was exhausted after a long trip and just wanted to rest up before his meeting. He had been promised a nonsmoking room, but his nose detected stale cigarette smoke. There it was—the wastebasket had not been emptied. In fact, he wondered if the room was even cleaned.

Henry thought this was only slightly better than trying to check in and learning your reservation isn't being honored. He reviewed his choices. He was too tired to argue but was angry at being mistreated. He could let it go and vow that his organization will no longer patronize this hotel chain. He knew he ought to speak up. But what if he was told there aren't any other rooms? What could he say to the registration clerk?

THE GOAL
Receive what you reserved or be bumped upward.

THE PLAN
1. *Insist on your due.* Show your confirmation notice, the price, and other details of the transaction. Be polite, but adamant about the hotel honoring its commitment.
2. *Go over the clerk's head.* If it's obvious the registration clerk can't (or won't be bothered or doesn't have authority to) help you, ask to speak to the manager.
3. *Listen carefully to the explanation.* But hold your ground. Keep smiling and repeating that you want the agreement honored. Then ask what can be done to resolve the difficulty.

4. *Explain alternatives available to you both.* Agree that you both want the same outcome—a satisfied customer. It costs a hotel very little to upgrade your room, especially if the better room is vacant anyway. Hold as a last resort the threat that you'd report the shoddy service to his superior and transfer your company's business elsewhere.

THE SCRIPT

YOU.   [*friendly*]. Good evening, Mr. Upton. I'm Henry Holloway. I'm sorry to impose on your time; however, I find myself in a predicament and I need your help. My reservation was specifically for a nonsmoking room. I am highly allergic to smoke and I can't stay in the room assigned to me.

MANAGER.   I'm terribly sorry, but unfortunately all our other rooms are occupied, as the registration clerk explained to you.

YOU.   I can appreciate your dilemma. Would I be correct in saying that we both have the same goal—a satisfied customer?

MANAGER.   Yes, of course.

YOU.   Then let's discuss what we can do to resolve this difficulty. Isn't it true that you keep a suite or two in reserve for special patrons?

MANAGER.   Yes, that's our policy.

YOU.   Then I suggest you move me into a suite, at the

same rate, of course, as the room I reserved that you are unable to provide.

MANAGER. Well, really, I—

YOU. We both want this to be resolved amicably. I don't want to detail shoddy service to your president as the reason my firm will no longer patronize your hotel. Mr. Upton, I really would appreciate your help in this situation.

MANAGER. All right, Mr. Holloway. We'll change your room to the suite. I'm sure you'll be very comfortable there.

GUIDELINE
Have your remedy in mind before complaining about the service.

34. Excuse Me— Do You Want My Business?

When store clerks and other workers ignore your needs

You've heard that poor service in the United States has been dubbed a national nightmare. And you've certainly experienced inexcusable treatment at the hands of repairmen coming to your home or clerks at stores you patronize.

You stopped by the hardware store to pick up a part you had ordered for your vacuum. The clerk smiled and said, "Can I help you?" That was the last conversation you had with anyone for eight minutes and twenty seconds. That's because as you were about to reply to the clerk, the telephone rang. He answered it, and you were left cooling your heels at the counter. If he were alone in the store, it might have been more tolerable. But there were two other workers putting things on shelves, also ignoring you, as you stood there. And from what you overheard, the telephone call sounded like a personal one.

You needed that part or you would have stomped out of there. You used to enjoy coming to that store. Now you're in a fury just trying to control your temper until you get the needed part.

THE GOAL
Negotiate reciprocal respect and consideration.

THE PLAN
1. *First try to win over the clerk.* You like this store and chances are you'll experience similar treatment elsewhere. Chewing out the clerk, while giving you momentary relief, won't get you better service next time. Make his day with a sincere compliment. You'll both feel good as you help him raise his self-concept.

2. *Talk to the owner or manager.* Anyone who wants to stay in business should know that the customer is the first priority. But sometimes the problem begins with management—poor hiring practice and training of workers, low pay, little respect, or no recognition or feedback. If managers treated employees better, employees would treat customers better.

3. *Avoid arguing. Swallow hard.* Remember, if you start by finding fault, he'll get defensive and resentful and it will be more difficult for you to shop there again. Instead, suggest to the manager how to meet your mutual interests.

THE SCRIPT

YOU.	[*beginning friendly, calling him by the name on his tag*]. You know, Harley, I've always enjoyed shopping here and most of the time I've received excellent service [*showing genuine warmth*].
HARLEY.	Really?
YOU.	Yes. I understand you've been busy and put in long hours. [*Use your insight to show understanding of his job.*] Yet you certainly know the merchandise and I've always found you to be patient. [*All workers want to feel their being there makes some difference.*]
HARLEY.	I try, but some of the customers are rude when they demand speedy service. That's more important to them than quality. We don't get respect from anyone. [*He knows you know he kept you waiting and appreciates your not mentioning it.*]
YOU.	I know how that hurts. Tell me, Harley, did the part I ordered for my vacuum ever come in?
HARLEY.	It sure did. I'll have it for you in a second. [*He practically leaps over the counter to get it. Next time you can be sure he'll remember you.*]

• • •

YOU.	[*to the manager*]. I'm glad you were able to get that part I needed for my vacuum.
MANAGER.	Well, we try to please our customers.

YOU.   I'm sure you do. I know how important it is these
            day to keep your steady customers from going over
            to the competition. I read somewhere about com-
            panies that survey customers to learn what they
            regard as important.

MANAGER.   That's interesting.

YOU.   Well, this article was saying how customers can be
            abusive at times.

MANAGER.   You'd be surprised what we have to deal with!

YOU.   Have you considered training clerks what to say to
            unreasonable demands?

MANAGER.   Well, you know every store has to have its rules.

YOU.   That's true. But, for example, when I hear "No, we
            can't do that, it's against policy," I'd much prefer
            being offered an alternative. And when your clerks
            are busy, maybe you could train and empower
            your stock people to use their good judgment
            when responding to customer needs? Is that a pos-
            sibility?

MANAGER.   You've given me a lot to think about. Thanks.

GUIDELINE

Restore self-esteem rather than get an unresponsive clerk fired.

Showing understanding starts a good relationship. And, as Lincoln
advised, it's better to give your path to a dog than be bitten by him
while contesting your rights.

35. If You Insist on Talking Down to Me...

*Responding to condescending
people paid to serve you*

Although it's your money being spent, you aren't getting your money's worth if you have to endure a haughty attitude.

You may be a baby boomer, but you never got around to learning about computers. You figured it was time you caught up. So you went to a large computer store and started asking questions of a salesperson to determine the differences among the many models.

The salesperson made you feel stupid because you had such a limited grasp. He appeared to be more concerned with flouting your ignorance than with sharing his knowledge. You had experienced a similar attitude the week before in a restaurant known for its French cuisine. You questioned the waiter, politely, about several dishes. His replies were snippy, as if you should have already known the answers. In both cases, you felt intimidated and offended but held your tongue. Now you feel that was a mistake and want to know what to say the next time this happens to you.

THE GOAL

Handle offenders firmly and forcefully, but friendly.

It's the same as dealing with a spoiled child.

THE PLAN

1. *Expect respect.* If you're offended by the treatment, say so. Forget the gracious smile. Be firm and direct but civil. Don't let your anger show through, or the intimidator is in control. Watch your body language. Try to relax if you find yourself making a fist or tensing your back.

2. *Remind yourself the other person has the problem.* You're being polite, so he obviously is the one who's troubled by someone or something that has nothing to do with you. This doesn't excuse the attitude, but it will help you connect with the condescender and get the information you want.

3. *Contact a higher level.* After you've tried to have a normal conversation and the offense continues, ask to speak to the owner or manager. You might want to follow up with a letter to the president of the company, briefly detailing the incident.

THE SCRIPT

YOU.   [*smiling, be friendly*]. Look here, I've asked you politely for information you should be happy to share with a customer. Is there some problem?

SALESMAN.   I'm answering your questions. What more do you want?

YOU.   I can only guess that you've had a bad day.

SALESMAN.   That's putting it mildly.

YOU.   Maybe we can start over. I need certain information that you have. I'm sure you can give it to me in a courteous manner. Would you like to try again?

• • •

YOU.   [*to the manager, just the facts, without emotion*]. I came here tonight to purchase a computer, but your salesperson seems reluctant to share his knowledge with me. Is there someone else who can assist me?

GUIDELINE

Condescenders lose their power if you don't cower.

You won't feel intimidated if you remind yourself that your offender would be a lost soul trying to do what you do so well.

36. Either We Work This Out, or You're Out a Customer

When they won't soften strict policies to accommodate you

When the rules are intractable, polish your persuasion skills.

After trying on eighteen outfits, you still couldn't quite make up your mind. The exhausted saleswoman had now invested an hour and a half with no sale. You explained that you really like the green suit, but the buttons bother you.

She shrugged off your concern, reminding you the suit was on sale, 50 percent off, and they don't change the buttons. Besides, she added, that's the design. It looks good that way.

While she failed to suggest a couple of modifications you could easily accomplish, she did say you could exchange the suit if you changed your mind. So you took home the suit and now you're unhappy.

The next morning you pack up the suit and your receipt and go back to ask for an exchange. But the customer service clerk points to the sign No Returns on Sale Items. She refuses to accept the suit.

THE GOAL
Have the store make an exception to their policy.

THE PLAN
1. *Find the decision-maker.* Don't argue with a clerk who doesn't have the power to authorize policy changes. (Depending on the situation, you keep going up a level until you find the one who *can* help you.)

2. *Come across as friendly, cooperative, and reasonable.* After you explain what happened, you're sure the owner will want to modify the policy for mutual satisfaction.

3. *Present yourself as a person with a problem.* You want them to identify with your dilemma. Ask for help and advice in solving it. Don't insult or blame anyone. Point up the benefits in seeking a solution rather than threatening revenge.

4. *Discuss your other options as a last resort.* Imply that, of course, neither of you would want you, for example, to file a complaint of misrepresentation to the Better Business Bureau or to write a letter to your local newspaper's consumer action column or advise your many friends about your predicament.

THE SCRIPT

DESK.   This suit was on sale. There are no refunds.

YOU.   I wasn't asking for a refund, but for an exchange. I was told I could exchange the suit if I decided it wasn't right for me.

DESK.   There is nothing here in the sales receipt that says you can do that. All sales are final. It says so right here. Do you see that sign?

YOU.   Yes. Now I want to speak to the owner.

• • •

Solomon Says:

Five negotiating tips:

1. Listen carefully, nodding to show you understand. Concentrate on what seems to be important and observe the body language.

2. Pretend you're the other person. Ask yourself, "If I were, what would I really want?"

3. Determine what you can offer to help meet that goal in exchange for getting what you want.

4. Involve your opponent in your suggestion. ("How would you feel about…?") Be concise; together, you can fill in the blanks.

5. Be straightforward with a self-confident attitude you may not yet feel.

YOU.	Hello, I'm Mrs. Leonard. You have such beautiful clothes here that when I came in yesterday, I had difficulty deciding on a suit.
OWNER.	Yes, we do have quite a variety on sale.
YOU.	Perhaps I misunderstood, but I was sure the saleswoman told me I could exchange this suit if I changed my mind.
OWNER.	That's our policy on regular sales, but on the discounted merchandise, there are no credits or exchanges.
YOU.	I understand why you would have to have such a policy, but I'm asking you to please help me with my problem. It's the buttons on this suit that bother me. I realized after I got it home that it'd cost too much to replace them. I'm never going to be happy wearing the suit as it is. What do you suggest we might do? I'm sure you can help me.
OWNER.	I'm sorry, but—
YOU.	We both benefit when you have a satisfied customer. The exchange won't cost you anything. I might even pick out a more expensive item. That would surely be a better solution than my other options.
OWNER.	Hmmm. . . . Yes, it would. Since there was a misunderstanding, I'll authorize the exchange.

GUIDELINE

Reach out—offer a solution that meets mutual needs.

You won't have to talk anybody into anything if you let them convince themselves.

Chapter VII

Teachers

High tech continues to drive the economy. You realize the need to keep your skills updated, especially cutting-edge technical proficiency and increasingly important people skills.

Downsizing and restructuring taught a difficult lesson: Each one is responsible for his or her own career. And there are still layoffs and mergers. You want to be able to move into a new job if it becomes necessary.

So you're taking advantage of a training program offered by your organization, or the course was in lieu of a pay raise. Or you're attending classes on your own after work. Or perhaps you're still in high school or college taking trade-related courses while working a job in the afternoon or evening.

Now you find that not all people with certificates are good teachers. Some don't know how to adjust the pace or won't stop to clarify a point, or they get angry if you question their opinions. Others look at you as though you're too dumb to figure it out. Whether your problem is with an egotistical college professor, a mean-spirited high school teacher, or an incompetent business instructor, your advancement, company refund, or graduation depends on your grade. You panic and want the right to question the grading system.

And you'll be darned if you can figure out how to talk to a teacher who's making your life a living hell.

37. Did You Know You Were Speeding in a School Zone?

When instructors go too fast and get mad if you ask questions

Your instructor knows her stuff, but she can't explain it in simple terms. She's arrogant and egotistical and makes you feel you're non compos mentis if you can't keep up.

To her, a question isn't part of learning, it's an interruption. Rigid, extremely demanding, and short of patience, she cuts you short when you ask for a simple explanation.

The worst part is that she jumps from one thought to the next without completing the first one. Her vague talk and incomplete sentences and phrases make it very difficult to follow.

You feel you're at a disadvantage. You desperately need a good grade. The tuition you paid out will be refunded by your company only if you get a B or better. Of course that's no skin off her nose. She runs the course the way she wants, apparently with little accountability.

You say you're becoming a nervous wreck.

THE GOAL
Increase your comprehension.
Once you do, the good grade will come automatically.

THE PLAN
1. *Put the onus on yourself.* Express the problem as one for which you are to blame. By making the ineptness yours, not the teacher's, you allow her to save face and help you.

2. *Be polite when you jump in.* Wait until she takes a natural pause—don't interrupt in the middle of a point. Then pull her back before she moves on to the next unrelated thought.

3. *Query other students.* Can you find a compatible few who express similar frustration? Consider joining forces.

4. *Seek a private talk.* If you choose the classroom to criticize her methods, she will resent it and become more hostile. You would be putting her in the embarrassing position of having to defend her authority. When you discuss the problem in her office after class, don't grovel. Be extremely tactful in questioning her opinion and asking for help. Asking, not telling, is a way to show respect.

Solomon Says:

A couple of hints on requesting help:

- Avoid disaster. Admit it when you can't do something and need a little guidance, instead of saying you can do it, then don't for fear of falling on your face.
- Show your willingness to work hard. You're just asking for a push in the right direction.

THE SCRIPT

PROF. [*in class*]. It is important for you to understand the difference between control and controls. . .For management the two words have different meanings, which reminds me I want to discuss with you the measurements we use to—

YOU. [*interrupting*]. Ms. Quinn, I'm confused. May I try to rephrase what you said to see if I have it straight in my mind? Is control the expectation and controls the means to get it?

PROF. [*angrily*]. Yes, that's right. Now as I was saying before I was interrupted. . .

• • •

YOU. [*after class, alone with the teacher*]. Ms. Quinn, I'd like to explain to you that I'm nervous. I wasn't trying to be disrespectful in class. It's just that I'm very concerned about passing this course. If I offended you, please excuse me.

PROF. No, that's all right. I expect you to question me if you don't understand something.

• • •

YOU. [*in her office with a few classmates*]. Several of us were thinking about meeting regularly as a study group. Do you think that's a good idea?

PROF. Yes, if you're capable of self-discipline.

YOU. Would you be willing to suggest other material that could bring us up to speed?

PROF. You appear to be serious. Okay, I'll help you.

GUIDELINE
Claim the blame to get more cooperation.

Act as though the difficulty is with your comprehension rather than with the teacher's techniques.

38. Because You're Considered an Expert in This Field...

Challenging opinions of instructors who are know-it-alls

With some teachers, you're not supposed to think, just absorb.

Your professor has tenure. Maybe because he has a lifetime guarantee he thinks he can be as nasty and resentful—not to mention inflexible—as he wants to be. Nobody evaluates or measures his effectiveness.

He conducts his lectures as though he's Chief Justice of the Supreme Court. Except a courtroom has decorum and he is rude and abusive.

He cuts you short if you venture an opinion. Speak out in class and you get ripped to shreds.

His negative methods aim at conformity and control. His only concern seems to be how results reflect upon him, with little respect for students as human beings. There's no room to get a better understanding and grow.

You feel stuck. He's the only one who teaches this required course. You're asking yourself how you're going to get through this term.

THE GOAL

Handle intimidation without offending your teacher.

THE PLAN

1. *Stop any frontal charge.* It sounds too much like you're trying to show up the teacher. And if so, that's perceived as offensive.

2. *Convert your remarks into questions.* Disagree by asking his opinion. When there's a lot of material to cover through lectures, that hall is not the place to tell what you think. Take a few seconds to jot down your question before asking it so that you don't falter. Then speak up in a loud, confident voice.

3. *Tap into your teacher's area of vulnerability.* He wants to be well regarded. That's the spot where you can reach him.

Solomon Says:

Four reminders to survive omnipotent teachers:

1. Don't argue. If they perceive you're criticizing them or not respecting their authority, they'll bombard you with more nasty darts.

2. Change the atmosphere. Appear unemotional and non-threatening, but maintain your self-respect. Don't whimper or apologize profusely.

3. Ask questions tactfully. If you don't verbally salute, they'll try harder to control you through fear and intimidation.

4. Learn what the teachers want—in what form and when. Then do assignments their way—there's no other way to get through the course.

THE SCRIPT

YOU. Professor Bright, would you mind expounding your theory, perhaps giving us a few specifics? Would it have the same effect if. . .? Would you please explain a little more why doing that would hurt. . .? Because you're considered an expert in this field, it would help us to know if you'd ever consider doing (c) instead of (b)?

GUIDELINE

You can show respect without kowtowing.

39. Is My Grade Open for Discussion?

How to question a grading system that appears irrational

Some instructors don't muzzle, they just puzzle you.

You feel you're not being treated fairly. Not just you; your classmates also are complaining about your instructor's rigidity. He charges the entire class with slacking off. To compensate, he's really piling on the work and is exceptionally rough on the grades.

You have already met all your undergraduate requirements, and this music appreciation elective was supposed to be relaxing. It's turned out to be a nightmare with the Instructor General threatening you by dangling the grades.

You're anxious to work hard to keep up your grade average so that you'll be accepted into a graduate program.

What can you do or say to change the situation?

THE GOAL

Have your grades based on effort and performance.

THE PLAN

1. *Make an appointment with your teacher.* Explain, in private, most politely and calmly but with determination, how the situation appears to you. Ask how to improve it. Listen carefully to the response. Your teacher may welcome a chance to spill out his frustrations with the class.

2. *Go to a higher up.* If the answer you get still doesn't make sense, write a brief factual account to the department head or administrator. Your dean may be able to arrange a transfer to another class.

3. *Organize a student letter-writing campaign.* Each of you send your epistle by registered mail to the teacher's superior or board to whom he has to report. Learn the complaint process in your school. You're not trying to get the instructor fired; you just want fair treatment.

4. *Follow other available appeal procedures.* Many colleges today make wide use of student evaluations in deciding to grant tenure, promotion, or salary increase. Fairness in grading often appears on a rating form. Critics say the forms may be misused and fail to distinguish between tough and easy courses, but they're generally regarded as a good measure of teaching ability.

Solomon Says:

Three tactics for dealing with overbearing authoritarians:

1. Mobilize—find others who are similarly affected.

2. Strategize—what would make the situation more palatable?

3. Compromise—how can you meet the teacher halfway?

THE SCRIPT

YOU.
Dr. Stone, if you have a few minutes, I'd appreciate being able to talk to you. Frankly, I'm at a loss to understand my grade from the last exam and it would help if you'd explain it to me. Also, with the majority of the class failing, do you consider it a fair test?

DR. STONE.
I would agree that it was a difficult test. But anyone who studied sufficiently should not have had trouble.

YOU.
Is it your policy to adjust the scores and grade on the curve?

DR. STONE.
You students have been coddled long enough. You're not in high school anymore.

YOU.
I know some of the students aren't taking the course seriously. What if a senior needed to maintain a grade average to be accepted into a graduate program in an unrelated area—would you reconsider adjusting the grade? Or perhaps allowing me to take another test?

DR. STONE.   It's over. I think you should stop obsessing and move on.

YOU.   You're right. I don't mean to minimize the value of your music appreciation course. But I'm nervous because I'm constantly under pressure. If I don't maintain my A average, I won't get accepted. I know you want to be regarded as fair when students fill out the evaluation forms [*his area of vulnerability*].

DR. STONE.   Of course. I've been a little tough on your class because many of the students obviously signed up thinking it was a snap course.

YOU.   Dr. Stone, although it's not my major, I love music, and I'm willing to work hard. I'll gladly do any extra work you assign in order to raise my grade and protect my chances of getting into my graduate program.

DR. STONE.   I'm going to have to think this over. I will reevaluate my last exam. If I decide it was too difficult, I'll arrange a substitute test.

GUIDELINE

Reason and persuasion are your best bets.

Seeking recourse from the department head is iffy. The teacher and his supervisor may be buddy-buddies. Be careful.

40. This Isn't Payback Time: You're Paid to Teach Me

When you're the target of an inexplicable vendetta

And then there are instructors you feel rather certain are expressing joy, in fact a maliciousness, in catching you in an error no matter how minuscule.

You're clueless as to the cause of the animosity. Dr. A. seems determined to make you suffer for some apparent misbehavior. Maybe it's a payback for suggesting how the class could be made more interesting. Or is she aiming to highlight her own stature rather than helping you, her student? Obviously, exposing your mistakes or putting you down by labeling your questions as ridiculous elevates her mood. The sarcastic look is worse than her words. You're sure she enjoys sadistic pleasure by embarrassing you in front of the group.

Nevertheless, your fate is in her hands. You need the new management skills to move ahead and must pass the course for the advanced degree—a key to getting the executive position you are hankering for. How can you deal with mean-spirited, cruel, and overly critical behavior that seems to stem from a personal vendetta?

THE GOAL

Win over the teacher.

THE PLAN

1. *Learn the precise demands of this instructor.* Go back to your notes from the first day of class when she probably spelled out her expectations. If you don't know precisely, check with fellow students. Or drop by her office to introduce yourself and clarify. If you don't ask, you can't complain.

2. *Improve your listening and observing skills.* You're not on an equal level. Forget trying to analyze your teacher's personality or trying to humiliate her, and get help with your study habits.

3. *Remain positive by framing reasonable questions.* Don't get defensive when you feel you're being needled. If possible, agree generally to her statements rather than take them as personal criticism.

THE SCRIPT

YOU.	Dr. Anderson, I've come by to ask you what, exactly, do you expect from the students? Or more to the point, what is it that I can do to be a better student?
DR. ANDERSON.	Students who expect to pass this course would not submit a report without correcting grammatical errors.
YOU.	Yes, professor, I agree. [*Assume this was a general comment. You're careful with written work. If she's referring to you, she'll have to come right out and say so.*] I'm afraid I may have gotten off on the wrong foot with you. Whatever I've done that may have offended you, please tell me so that I can apologize.
DR. ANDERSON.	You insulted my ability to convey information effectively, and there was no way I would debate that with you in front of the class.
YOU.	I am very sorry that I misspoke and ask you to forgive my insensitivity. Now that I put my foot in my mouth, please tell me how I can take it out.
DR. ANDERSON.	I expect students to understand that there isn't time to debate every contrasting view. That's best explored in special reports they take the trouble to research and which I am glad to read and reconsider.

GUIDELINE

It may be your own bias that needs to be set straight.

If you want to make the grade, prepare to accept the authority of those who control the outcome.

Part B

Personal Relationships

Poor communication is at the core of most personal relationship problems.

When it comes to your peers, you're supposed to be on the same level, with no one having authority over the other. Maybe so, but that doesn't stop irritating, brazen, arrogant, and presumptuous behavior. You find yourself flabbergasted when humiliating spouses, bullying exes, pushy relatives, ear-splitting neighbors, and hurtful friends try to control you.

If you're dealing with people who are dependent on you, it's a tricky skill to hold the reins firmly without choking creativity. Workers and teenage kids may resent not only their dependence, but also your power over them. You are micromanaging if you make or spell out every possible procedure—and this is stifling. However, you can decrease hassles by allowing them some say, for example, in the rule-establishing process.

Part B stresses ways to give and get respect.

Chapter VIII

Spouses and Significant Others

C'mon, let's admit it. No sooner do you agree to be partners than you try to change the other individual. In going from independence to couplehood, there's a tremendously strong temptation to try to transform your partner into the way you believe one ought to be or act or feel.

If you don't conform to the other's idea, your partner could be hurt and seek revenge. Somehow you're to blame. Somehow you're wrong. You may be charged with unfounded ulterior motives. Or become the target of a lover who enjoys humiliating you. The criticism can be incessant.

Sometimes the root of the trouble is a failure to say how *you* feel or not checking if you misunderstood or misinterpreted the situation. It's normal to have feelings and important that both positive and negative ones are expressed.

Whether you're arguing about money, children, housekeeping duties, social activities, making plans without telling you (the list is endless), it's essential that you agree on what the quarrel is about. Then if you can resist ducking a fight or walking out in the middle of one, you have the chance to be creative in deciding what to do about the problem. You could start by taking a cue from business and define a mission statement for your relationship.

41. Let's Be Fair— You Do Your Share

Balancing the load when you're being overburdened

Too frequently, the trouble starts from feeling imposed upon.

You're building up a head of steam. You both have jobs, so you both do the housework. But how could Gail be so inconsiderate? She knew you wanted to watch the game on TV, but she insisted that you finish washing the windows first.

Gail goes out with her friends while you're at home balancing the checkbook. How did it come about that you got stuck putting the laundry in the washer and dryer? And the list of complaints goes on.

You don't want to fight, so you keep on doing what you're doing but feel you're being used. You resent the lack of respect for your time. However, saying nothing appears to make matters worse. You're thinking about going on strike. Maybe that would make her feel guilty.

THE GOAL
Redistribute chores for a fairer workload.

THE PLAN
1. *Realize your partner's no mind reader.* Determine to speak up. Gail may not be aware how this situation is affecting you. By your not letting her know you feel imposed upon, she probably assumes things are OK the way they are. If you *don't* say something, the problem isn't with her, it's with you.

2. *List all the tasks for the week.* Scratch any that aren't absolutely necessary. Note alongside each item an estimated amount of time it takes. Be fair and include everything each of you does.

3. *Find the right time to have a discussion.* Talk about the stress you both carry home with you after work. Explain the problem as you see it. This is your partner, not your opponent. You can reveal your feelings without accusing her of being selfish. Ask for her ideas in resolving the issue. Then add your suggestions. Negotiation starts when you identify shared concerns. This narrows the scope.

4. *Agree on a new plan.* Mark by each item who is responsible for what or if you are going to rotate any assignments. What you decide isn't as important as both of you having an equal voice in making the decision and then in abiding by it. And when your partner does take over a chore you used to do, accept the way it's done even though it doesn't meet your standards.

Solomon Says:

To share the load:

- DON'T apologize for not being able to do it all.

- DON'T fight or accuse. Keep this an impersonal, procedural discussion to explore a better way.

- DO crystallize priorities before you start splitting the tasks.

THE SCRIPT

YOU.   Gail, is this a good time to talk? [*She nods in agreement.*] I've been feeling increasingly annoyed lately. It seems to me I'm stuck with an unfair amount of the work around the house.

GAIL.   Well, if you feel that way, why didn't you say something?

YOU.   I know I should have spoken sooner. But now I'd like to ask you what you think we could do about this.

GAIL.   [*defensively*]. I thought I was doing my share.

YOU.   I'm sure you do, Gail. But look at the list of things that have to be done each week and the time each takes. Read this to see if my approximations are accurate.

GAIL.   This looks about right.

YOU.   Then let's initial every chore that each of us will be doing.

GAIL. Gee, I really hadn't realized. Look here, we could
switch. . .and I could do. . . What do you think?

GUIDELINE

*Don't wilt—tilt. Present the data that matters and let the evidence speak
for itself.*

42. Clue Me In
So We Can Both Decide

*When major decisions are made
without consulting you*

Sharing the workload is easy compared to sharing significant determinations.

Lyle, your husband, takes actions that affect both of you without talking it over first or thinking things through. His attitude is that he knows what's best.

Your main problem is the money he spends. All your life, you've always had to budget carefully. Now you have a spouse who spends without a plan from your joint checking account. Screaming and accusations only produce denials.

Lyle makes checks payable to cash so that you don't know what he's bought and later, you suspect, he lies about it. You tried making him feel guilty and, as a result, he just hides his purchases from you.

Now it seems the more you preach, the less he hears you. You think he's being juvenile and you don't know what to do.

THE GOAL
Convince your spouse to acknowledge the problem.
Persuade him to offer his ideas for resolving it.

THE PLAN
1. *Discuss your personal histories.* Your diverse approaches to monetary matters are probably imbedded from childhood and may explain your differing attitudes today. You won't change your spouse's basic money personality, but you can try to understand it.

2. *Probe for a hidden, deeper conflict.* A fight over money may be rooted in unspoken anger or resentment over, for example, lack of attention or the need to feel in control.

3. *Plan and record your joint monetary goals.* This includes what you both agree is important and when you hope to do what.

4. *Prepare a divided budget.* Work out a plan (some couples need separate bank accounts) that lets each of you spend x dollars without reporting to the other. Earmark some funds for your individual goals but set a limit on the amount either spends without talking it over first.

5. *Use a joint account for regular monthly household expenses.* Remember, you're in this together.

THE SCRIPT

YOU. Lyle, when we got married, we promised that we'd share everything.

LYLE. Yeah, I think we do pretty much.

YOU. Sometimes it seems we're doing things your way without discussing it. Like your accepting the transfer without consulting me or buying the new TV without telling me.

LYLE. Here we go again. Now what's eating you?

YOU. I'm really worried that we're overspending.

LYLE. Then we'll just delay payments a month.

YOU. No, I'm sorry, I can't do that. [*Explain without accusing.*] I grew up in a family that paid bills the minute they were due. It upsets me when we're late. I guess that wasn't ingrained in you, right?

LYLE. Yeah, with my folks, whenever we had extra cash, we celebrated. We enjoyed life without worrying over each penny we spent.

YOU. Well, that explains a lot. But now how are we going to pay our bills on time and still have money for some extras? What do you think we can do to get back on track?

LYLE. I guess we need two budgets or maybe two separate accounts. From now on, you pay the bills since that gets you so antsy. Then we'll divide what's left between us. I need some money I can spend without accounting to you for it.

YOU. That sounds great. It's what we both need. But I think we should also plan to save a small percentage every payday. Is that okay with you?

GUIDELINE

Dig below the surface—anger and resentment may be disguised.

Controlling money is a frequently veiled way to get even. Or sometimes there's a clash stemming from different cultural backgrounds that needs to be exposed and hashed out.

43. I've Never Been So Embarrassed

Stopping humiliation, especially in front of others

Another form of control shows up in partners who like to puncture the other's pride.

That's Beatrice. You recognize that look of glee as your significant other watches you squirm in front of your friends or family. She sees nothing wrong in hitting you where you're vulnerable or making you look foolish by shredding your dignity.

It's often an unexpected shot, and to try to defend yourself would only make the embarrassment greater. So you smile silently during the incident when you really want to tell her to shut up.

You don't know why she delights in revealing your personal problems to other people. You feel bad enough about going bald or gaining weight without her broadcasting it. When you asked her how someone who's supposed to care for you could treat you like that, her response was that you exaggerate, that you can't take a joke and are oversensitive.

Tired of lugging the weight of indignation and resentment, you lashed out demanding that she stop making a fool of you. This led to a big argument and nothing was resolved.

THE GOAL
Curb the humiliation.

THE PLAN
1. *Exercise your choice.* It's up to you to stay negative or to switch to a positive approach. Stop feeling sorry for yourself. Being angry and blaming your partner is just consuming too much of your energy.

2. *Stop playing her game.* Change from the angry way you've been reacting and you'll stop feeling victimized. Admittedly, it's darn hard to stay composed when you feel you've been struck unfairly. But since you believe she's behaving badly, regain control by demonstrating that you refuse to be intimidated by her.

3. *Go along with the joke.* Try topping her by going one better. ("How bald am I? I am *so* bald that people are always using my shiny head for a mirror.")

4. *Zing her back.* Deftly and politely jab her with your prepared responses. She shouldn't mind because she sees nothing wrong with personal digs. If she does, that should teach her to stop. The aim isn't to win a competition, but to resolve the problem.

5. *Simply exit.* Leave her there to explain why. Don't stay still and suffer. Do something! Even walking away is making a statement.

Solomon Says:

Did you know…

…If you don't speak up when you're being tormented, you're giving others silent approval to keep on doing what they're doing?

…It's easier to learn the underlying reason for the attacks and get your partner to be direct with criticism if you counter cruelty with courtesy?

…You can begin a real discussion if you go ahead and admit your feelings   an honest statement, not an accusation?

THE SCRIPT

BEA. Don't feel hurt. [*Expecting you to feel the way she thinks you ought to.*] You know you have to learn how to take a joke. You're just too sensitive.

YOU. Perhaps. [*Admitting to yourself there's a grain of truth to that.*] But you should know that people have different levels of sensitivity. To you, it's a game; to me, it's a pain. [*Explaining your feelings—no hiding the hurt.*] And I won't continue taking that kind of abuse.

BEA.   Aw, c'mon, grow up.

YOU.   Okay, but I'm giving you fair warning. The next time
       you humiliate me in front of our friends, I'm going to
       tell a few secrets about you that you'd prefer be kept
       under wraps. That should be a good test of *your* ability
       to take a joke.

GUIDELINE
   Toss back what you can't accept.

   Without anger, you can enjoy the success from a humorous
approach. Or, when you feel intimidated, just return the ball to your
partner's court.

44. Stop Nagging Me

*How to instantly stop
continual fault-finding*

Next is the spouse who dominates by unrelenting criticism.

When your wife isn't saying something negative, she's smirking or giving you a nasty look or rolling her eyes back. You can't do anything right, and you're sick and tired of taking her guff.

Whatever problem arises, Sally says you caused it. She goes on to tell you why you act the way you do or feel the way you feel, playing pop psychologist. You're always at fault, but she has the right answer: Just do what she wants. Sometimes the issues are petty and really not worth talking about. So you shrug it off. But other times you'd like to have a decent, respectful discussion—even a heated argument would be good—but that seems impossible.

THE GOAL
Put an end to the nagging.
Teach your partner that you have a right to be respected.

THE PLAN
1. *Choose your battles.* If the issue's not worth fighting over, saying "You may be right" will end the discussion. You haven't said she *is* right, but neither have you disagreed. Argument over. When you're the one bringing up a touchy matter, ask if it's a good time and allow enough time to talk.

2. *Reveal how you feel.* Speak up when you feel strongly, with no excuses or apologies. Unexpressed feelings fester. You have a right to your own individuality and she to hers.

3. *Out with it—don't duck or hint.* When you're nagged to death, say so. If you don't, it's a signal that you approve of the treatment you're receiving. Refuse to continue a conversation that doesn't show mutual respect. Ask for it, and if you don't get treated civilly, stop talking and move away.

4. *Lighten up.* Have fun with the fight. Smile as you disagree with humor, honesty, and civility.

5. *Listen raptly to the response.* Take off the blinkers to get a broader picture. Recognize that another point of view exists. Can you accept any of it? Concentrate on the points she repeats—that's most important to your partner. Feed this back in your own words to show you understand, even if you don't agree, rather than thinking about your countercharge.

6. *Clear the air.* Use a question rather than a declaration if you don't understand or you disagree. Consider points of agreement as well as differences. Decide what's reasonable to expect from each other and what's hitting below the belt.

THE SCRIPT

SALLY. You said you'd pick up a present for the party on your way home. You should feel ashamed for embarrassing me. Now what do I do? Tell the host my stupid husband isn't playing with a full deck?

YOU. Until we can talk politely, I'd rather not discuss my alleged forgetfulness.

SALLY. You make me so mad. I depend on you, but you're so self-absorbed, you never come through. What kind of a moron did I marry?

YOU. A pretty smart one.

SALLY. What I tell you is for your own good.

YOU. [*verbalizing her view*]. I know you want what's best for me, but it really hurts my feelings when I'm being pelted with continuous criticism. [*Telling what bugs you.*] When you're hurt, you probably don't realize what your sharp attacks do to me.

SALLY. Well, I don't understand why you can't see that you're wrong to—

YOU. As a couple, it's natural each of us does things that aren't the way the other one would. I'm not asking you to change your way, just to let me tell you how I feel. And instead of picking on each other, let's talk it over to settle our problems. Now, as for the party, I ordered champagne and they'll have it gift-wrapped for us to pick up on the way there.

SALLY. Oh, that's good. I guess I misjudged you.

GUIDELINE

You have a right to your opinion and your spouse has a right to be wrong.

If your spouse persists in squawking, insist the talking be a fair fight.

45. Please Talk to Me

Breaking the barrier when
you get the silent treatment

To some spouses, squawkers beat not talking at all.

You wish you could lasso your spouse to keep her from walking out in the middle of an argument. She'll fire accusations, then stalk off without waiting for your reply.

Or you come home and get an icy greeting. No explanation. You're in the dark and all you know is that she's ticked off. And she won't give you a clue as to why she's become an impenetrable clam.

Often it's something rather simple. Like the time you eventually learned that because you didn't call to say you'd be late, the dinner was all dried out.

You think she dummies up, stares daggers, or walks off just to manipulate you. She's mad and going to control you by extending the nonverbal attack. But you're still embarrassed by the silence, so you try to fill the communication void. No use. She stays mum and sulks until she's good and ready to talk to you after you've suffered enough for your "sin."

THE GOAL

Cease and desist the childish behavior.

Handle disagreements as a couple of adults.

THE PLAN

1. *Don't try to explain yourself.* When emotions are that strong, you don't want to say something you'll regret later. Simply acknowledge that she's upset and say you'll discuss it when she's calm enough for a civil discussion.

2. *Establish some ground rules.* When you're ready to talk, stop the accusations by agreeing that you're both responsible for creating an uncomfortable situation. People get angry for a zillion reasons. While it's fine to explain what makes you feel annoyed and how you were affected, there's no point in trying to analyze the other's actions. Unless they tell you, you really don't know what others are feeling.

3. *Work out a plan together.* Literally, write down your own rules of behavior. Examine what you have to do or change in order to adhere to your new rules.

4. *Set a date for a progress report.* Decide when you'll talk again to make any necessary adjustments.

Solomon Says:

Freeze to melt the ice when mum's the word with your partner!

Resist the temptation to keep talking in order to counteract the unbearable sound of silence. Don't apologize for what you supposedly did—you don't know what because your mate won't say. Now calmly pose questions that require more than a yes or a no to try to pry an answer out of those locked lips.

THE SCRIPT

You. Hi, honey, I'm home.

MEG. [*dripping with icicles*]. Hello.

You. What did I do now?

MEG. You know, and that's all I'm going to say.

You. Obviously you're mad about something. When you're ready to talk, let me know.

You. [*much later*]. Look here, there's no use tossing darts at one another. We have a situation that we probably both helped create and we both have to clear up.

MEG. Just read this letter that came today and you'll see why I'm so upset. You really goofed this time.

You. Okay, I understand your reaction. I made a mistake, but you don't have to rub my nose in it. And not talking to me for four hours doesn't help. Let's figure out how we want to handle our disagreements in the future. These will be our very own rules that you and I will write together.

MEG.   I guess that does make sense.

GUIDELINE
As a couple, establish your own personal rules of behavior.

When mum's the word, your spouse is using silence to control you. Agree on what's acceptable and unacceptable to you both.

46. This Isn't Getting Us Anywhere

*When a partner exaggerates
your faults with name-calling*

Another form of unfair fighting occurs when a soul mate provokes with offensive branding.

We all make mistakes, but your partner pins nasty labels on yours. If you forget to pick up the cleaning, you're stupid. If you're late, you're inconsiderate. If you didn't iron the T-shirts, you're lazy.

Dan takes one incident and blows it up until it's a character flaw. You love Mr. Perfect, but living with him is getting increasingly difficult.

The worse part is that when you get called derogatory names, you lose your temper and yell and scream trying to defend yourself. You feel ashamed of the way you react and the root cause of the disagreement never gets aired.

THE GOAL
Converse with a civil tongue.
Lower the barrier that's behind the apparent anger.

THE PLAN
1. *Refuse to walk into the maligner's trap.* You are being bullied, so change your response. You and Dan both know that you're not stupid, inconsiderate, lazy, or whatever else he brands you. As long as you continue giving excuses trying to defend yourself, your partner is controlling you and the situation.

2. *Go forward defining the real problem.* Change the focus. Explain there's no reason for the personal attack and ask what could be done to make things run more smoothly.

3. *Gain cooperation.* Show Dan a better way to get what he really wants.

THE SCRIPT

You.   OK, Dan, you're angry, so you're accusing me of doing something stupid. I don't intend to argue the point since we both know I am not stupid. I will not fight with you over that.

Dan.   Don't you think I have a right to be angry when you're so neglectful? It's your responsibility to see that—

You.   Wait a minute. Instead of calling each other names, which doesn't get us anywhere, let's look at what you're really angry about and try to fix it [*showing you do care about his problem but you don't like his attack*].

Dan.   You knew I wanted to wear that blue suit to the meeting tonight.

You.   Yes, I didn't forget. The cleaner was running behind schedule and it won't be ready until tomorrow. Now the question is, How can we try to avoid this kind of problem? What options do we have? Do we find another cleaner? Do we do a better job of planning ahead? What do you think we should do when we run into difficulties?

GUIDELINE

Watch your fighting manners—breeding is exposed by behavior in a quarrel.

Chapter IX

Your Ex

Some couples break up amicably. They've grown apart and realize it's time to move on. Many times, though, dissolving the relationship gets nasty. The enormous amount of unresolved hurt and anger fuels a feud that goes on forever.

Occasionally one partner may become compulsive. Be alert to danger signals. If you suspect your former spouse or lover is going off the deep end, don't wait for the problem to escalate. Get help immediately from professionals. Make the appropriate phone call: perhaps mental health hotlines to speak to counselors, abuse centers that are safe refuge for you and your children, or your lawyer to rush a restraining order from the court.

This chapter, however, is about run-of-the-mill nastiness—the kind of "normal" fighting you thought you'd be through with when you stopped being a couple. You're still miserable, at war, and you need a new suit of tactical armor.

47. It's Time to Move On

When your former partner refuses to let go

You couldn't work out your difficulties. Richard refused to go with you to a marriage counselor or even let you go by yourself. That, he reiterated, would harm his professional reputation. It would reflect poorly upon him as a college professor.

You tried but couldn't change the pattern. It was always your fault that he feels hurt. You didn't do what he told you to, so how was he going to explain your behavior to his family and peers? His alleged humiliation scraped the criticism off of him and piled it on you.

And even when he said he was sorry, he was unable to admit his rotten behavior. A defiant "I'm sorry you're angry" wasn't an apology but a manipulative verbal trick. The problem became your unreasonable anger which was *your* problem and *your* fault that he felt hurt.

Demanding came easily to Richard, who had grown up as the oldest sibling. As a husband, he got the idea that he was an infallible lord of his manor. When he added Ph.D. after his name, he lost whatever flexibility he previously had manifested.

After the last emotionally abusive fight, you needed to escape. The divorce gave little relief. The constant calls begging you to come back invariably end in a heated argument.

THE GOAL

Find a peaceful solution.

THE PLAN

1. *Seek professional help if you feel threatened.* Figure that the alarming behavior, despite apologies, not only won't diminish but more likely will intensify. Check listings in the phone book for resources mentioned in the chapter introduction.

2. *Remain firm and respectful.* When his behavior is nonthreatening but he continues to beg you to take him back, although you are determined not to, try a little more gentle touch.

3. *Concentrate on your own needs.* If you can't let go of the grudge, your ex wins—he's still controlling you. The more you can focus on positive thoughts, the sooner you'll be able to get going on your new life. If there are no children involved, there's no need to continue contact. Use an answering machine to monitor your calls and no longer be available to talk to him.

Solomon Says:

Three keys to escape your ex's guilt trap:

1. Be very clear about your feelings. ("As I've said many times, I [feel] [need]…")

2. Calmly recite the reality—just the facts with no interpretation, excuse, or apology. ("We want different things out of life.")

3. Make your ex accept responsibility for his or her choice of behavior. ("How you react to your family and friends is your decision. I am no longer involved. Good-bye and good luck.")

THE SCRIPT

RICH. I don't know what to say to people when they ask about you. I tell them you'll soon get over your anger and we can start again.

YOU. Richard, it's over. Please accept that. We can't be together anymore. I refuse to be scolded for everything I do and don't do.

RICH. Well, if you'd only listen to me, we could—

YOU. [*interrupting*]. No, we're not going that route any more. I have no desire to change you. You have a right to feel the way you do. At this point, it would seem that what you really require is a puppet that gladly lets you pull the strings. And if that's what you want, fine. I just can't be that pawn.

RICH. How could you embarrass me this way?

YOU. There's nothing for you to be embarrassed about. No one is to blame if two people think differently. You should know, however, that I have some very definite plans for my future so I won't be talking to you anymore. And I truly hope you'll find a way to enjoy the rest of your life. Good-bye.

GUIDELINE

No one takes advantage of you without your consent.

48. Your Threats Aren't Good for Our Kids

*How to handle bullying
and tyrannizing*

Some exes try to hold on to you with persistent pleas. Others try to retain control with threats.

You're still getting orders from Allison. Couple that with her domineering, unnerving tone and frigid stare. To keep the peace and not upset your son Peter, you're contemplating the best way to handle the ultimatums Ali keeps issuing.

Although you've split, you can see that she's still angry. You've concluded that she keeps trying to intimidate you because she's out for revenge. For example, Ali is making your allowed visitation very difficult. And she's spending more money than she should and then attacking you for denying your son the best of everything.

Allison plays upon your devotion to your son to snare you into doing things her way. You feel powerless to deal with her outrageous behavior. She keeps hatching plots, threatening to drag you back into court.

THE GOAL
Untie the manipulative bands.

THE PLAN
1. *Keep your face from reflecting emotion.* The darts she tosses at you have a terrible sting. But if you let this reaction show, she'll pounce even more. She's bullying you—don't stoop to her level and don't countercharge.

2. *Ask her to repeat her request.* React as though you couldn't believe what you just heard.

3. *Reassert your position.* Reiterate the agreement that was reached in court. Keep referring to it, firmly, politely, without giving an inch. If she continues dangling your son as the price for getting her way, just stop talking.

4. *Dummy up.* Give her a knowing smirk that says volumes.

Solomon Says:

Try this two-step with your intimidating ex:

- Let the bully land verbal blows without your interrupting. If you smile but say nothing, apparently unscathed, you win that round.

- Score a TKO by asking, "Do you hate me more than you love your kids? No? Then let's talk." Keeping communication open between you will help your children adjust to the divorce.

THE SCRIPT

ALI. You really don't care about your son or you'd see to it that Peter gets everything all his friends have.

YOU. [*smiling*]. I can't believe what you're asking that I buy for a nine-year-old boy. That's incredible! You're kidding, aren't you?

ALI. You know darn well I mean it.

YOU. Look, Ali, I'm not only living up to the court order, I'm always doing more than is required. From now on though, I'll just follow the letter of the agreement.

ALI. So, there you go, just as selfish as ever. You really don't give a damn about Peter's emotional happiness, do you?

YOU. [*dead silence; let your look say it all. I'm on to you and you're not going to get away with this anymore.*]

GUIDELINE

When a bully has you hog-tied, your strong, polite defiance dissolves the ropes.

49. They're Our Kids—
Not Our Weapons!

*When your ex tries to poison
the kids' minds against you*

Next we have the exes who intend to win, even if the price is using your own children as bargaining tools.

It was his weekend with the children and when your ex came to pick them up, he invited you to come with them to the circus. The kids, of course, joined in, hoping to have their family "whole" again. You refused nicely and politely and told them to have fun.

You thought no more about it until later. Back home, after their father left, the kids wanted to know why you were always so mean to their daddy. He was being so nice inviting you, but you refused to come.

He did it again! Another sneak attack.

He's systematically turning their little minds against you, using his own children as pawns in his sick game to get custody. How can you defend yourself against a lying finger pointer without becoming one yourself?

THE GOAL
Restore civility for the sake of the kids.

THE PLAN
1. *Take the children out of the middle.* The temptation is enormous, really overpowering, to tell the kids what you believe their father is really like. Oh, how you long to expose him for the liar and manipulator that he is! But don't. This would only hurt and confuse the children even more.

2. *Ignore the kids' parroting charges against you.* Reply simply that you're following the judge's orders.

3. *Prepare for a controlled private confrontation.* Role play with yourself, imagining the whole conversation. You can best respond to your ex's anger and intimidation by pointing up the consequences of his actions. As difficult as this is, force yourself to attack his behavior, not him personally. Practice with a tape recorder so that you can hear how you sound. Say it over and over again until you're sure you can look him in the eye and come across as calm and confident.

4. *Use the only leverage you have.* You can't give him what he wants, either to get back together or be awarded full custody of the children. If he persists in turning the kids against you, let him know you'll no longer be silent while he insists on playing devious games.

THE SCRIPT

SON. You don't have feelings for other people, Mom. You were being selfish not to come with us.

YOU. [*ignoring your ex's slimy tactics*]. I'm glad you had a good time with your father.

SON. But why didn't you come with us?

YOU. The judge ordered Daddy to visit alone with you, without me. I'm with you all week long. These visits are special times for you to be with your father.

YOU. [*privately, when the children can't hear you*]. Ed, our first consideration has to be what's best for the kids. We both have to help them adjust. The court gave you specific times to be with the children. Instead of using the kids to get back at me, why don't you just enjoy your time together?

ED. I don't know what you're talking about.

YOU. The kids were sad and nasty all during the week because of comments you made to them about me during your last visit. If we resort to undermining each other, the children are upset. They're too young to comprehend the tug of war between us.

ED. It's always my fault, isn't it? How about the schemes you've pulled?

YOU. [*ignoring the personal attack with a smile that says "I'm wise to your antics*"]. To keep the kids from becoming upset, do not invite me along on future visits. If I hear that you are using these visits to turn the children against me, I'll have to go back to the judge and ask for a remedy.

GUIDELINE
If words alone don't work, take action.
You can't allow your children to be brainwashed by warring parents.

50. Let's Be Fair

Reducing arguments about property settlement

One of the hardest parts about splitting up can be splitting possessions.

You're in the process of working out the details. Dividing the assets, you must decide what you keep and what Roz gets. Every time you think about it, you get mad. This is insanity and it feels as though it will never end.

Whenever you have a meeting, you're at each other's throats. You couldn't get along while you were together and it's worse now. Roz is totally demanding, trying to force you to choose when you feel you're entitled to have several of the items. She just won't listen to reason and wants all she can get her hands on.

THE GOAL
Retain possession of items most important to you.

THE PLAN
1. *Be explicit.* Prepare a list of what you want. Work out a system (for example, the number of stars) to indicate the order of your priorities.

2. *Understand how slowly legal wheels grind.* You can't make the process go faster, so you'll need more patience.

3. *Make one more last-ditch attempt.* Try to reason with your spouse, but if she continues with the either/or commands, toss them back at her with some either/ors of your own.

4. *If there's no progress, stop the direct talks.* If you have no conversations with your soon-to-be-ex, you won't feel victimized. This is why you have an attorney to represent you.

5. *Turn over the property division to your attorney.* Lawyers are used to the negotiating procedure. Have no more direct talks with your ex. Get busy doing other things to get your mind off the negotiation.

THE SCRIPT

YOU. Roz, before we meet again to divide the tangible items, let's see if a little advance preparation will help us reach an agreement. How about each of us listing those items we most want to keep, in order of importance to us?

ROZ. OK, but don't try to pull any fast ones on me.

YOU. Roz, it makes no sense. I play the piano and you don't. Why would you want to keep it?

ROZ. It's a beautiful piece of furniture that adds class to the living room. Besides, someday I may take lessons.

YOU. OK, then I'll take the sterling silverware and the good china.

ROZ. When are you going to entertain twelve people! That's ridiculous!

YOU. Maybe so, but they were gifts from my parents and I have a sentimental attachment.

ROZ. You're always trying to manipulate me.

YOU. Well, I think you'll agree we're getting nowhere. There's no point in continuing these talks. We'll let our attorneys work out the details.

GUIDELINE

Keep still and let your lawyers do the negotiating.

When you reach an impasse, stop banging your head against a steel door and allow your representatives to talk it over.

51. Let's Resolve This, or You'll Be Hearing from My Lawyer

Dealing with your ex's evading judicial decisions

You may no longer be together, but you're still dealing with lies and broken promises.

Eric, your ex-spouse, is a louse, a weasel, a chameleon. His excuses are nothing but bare-faced lies to justify his manipulative tactics.

He didn't send the child-support check, he said, because he was sick last week. But your neighbor bumped into him in the store and reported he looked fine to her. Or he was late in getting the children home because service at the restaurant was extraordinarily slow. (Two hours slow?) Eric has always lied through his teeth. You have trouble believing his explanations when he's been a deceitful, untrustworthy truth twister in the past. This irresponsible, flirting-with-the-truth habit is what led to your splitting up.

You're wondering if he ever intended to abide by his promise to pay child support in the first place. You won't be surprised when he finds a way to blame you for his problems.

THE GOAL

Persuade your ex to pull together with you.

THE PLAN

1. *Talk about mutual hopes for the children.* The need for them to feel safe and secure. Their minimum requirements.

2. *Discuss his problem.* The problem is his; don't let him make it "our" problem. Ask questions that require direct answers.

3. *Tap into his desires.* For example, he may be after more frequent and longer visitation rights. Discuss how he can achieve this.

THE SCRIPT

YOU. We've discussed this many times, so I know you want your kids to be fed, housed, and clothed properly. Didn't you agree to send a check twice a month for their support?

ERIC. Yes, I did. I was late because things come up and I can't always manage to be on time.

YOU. Eric, this is part of the agreement approved by the court. I'm sure if you put your mind to it, you could solve the problem.

ERIC. I do the best I can. I never seem to have enough money to take care of everything.

YOU. I do understand your difficulty. So how about starting with your first obligation—your children? Then you can budget what's left for your other concerns.

ERIC. I dunno how I'm gonna do that.

YOU. I'm sure you'll find a way. After all, you only have two choices: (1) if you don't pay on time, I'll ask the court to garnish your wages or (2) you show me that you're taking your responsibilities seriously, and I'll ask the judge to allow you to spend more time and have greater privileges. The children's needs must be met. The choice is up to you how that will come about.

GUIDELINE

You'll get more money from honey than from vinegar.

Sound understanding but firm in showing alternatives. If he feels he was somehow left out of the child-support decision, point out the relationship between improving current actions to improving future rulings.

Chapter X

Parents

Whether you live at home or have left the nest, have spouses and kids of your own, or give your parents financial or physical support, your parents remain authority figures to most of you.

You grew up expecting your parents to be perfect and were shocked—at times unforgiving—that they could make mistakes. Some of you still bear the emotional scars from hurtful parental comments and name-calling.

Other parents have trouble loosening the reins. They still mind your business and jump to conclusions. It seems most conversations end in an argument. Or you're drowning in guilt or unreasonable demands on your time.

Chapter X is about giving your parents the respect they deserve while staunchly defending your own independence.

52. I'm an Adult;
I Can Run My Own Life

When they interfere with the way you handle your decisions

You love your folks, but their noses are always in your personal business. You're choking on the prying questions followed by unsolicited advice incessantly crammed down your throat.

As you see it, they believe the job of parents is to control how their children act. It doesn't matter that you're an adult; they continue to cling to this strong sense of responsibility.

They still try to change your decisions because they are older and assumed to be wiser. You're supposed to listen and to obey their decrees of "You ought to. . ." "You should. . ." It doesn't stop with your life. They instruct you on how you must discipline your children. They undermine your rules when they baby-sit the grandkids. Why is it they were strict with you, but insist on spoiling your kids?

Your parents always were opinionated. Now it's worse. Whatever you espouse, only they know the gospel truth and you're dead wrong.

THE GOAL
Agree on ways to show mutual respect.

THE PLAN
1. *Hide a recorder.* Place it under the table the next time they come to dinner. When you play it back, they can hear themselves. Not just the words, but the tone, the force. That's your springboard to start a discussion.

2. *Reevaluate your position.* Is there enough validity to what they're saying to modify your stance? Or are you more convinced that yours is a good decision? The one advantage to hearing another opinion is forcing you to rethink yours and strengthen your belief.

3. *Assertively block the barrage of advice.* Stop giving them the ammunition that erodes your self-confidence. Stop trying to convince them that you're right and they're wrong—that's banging your head against the wall.

4. *Firmly state your belief in what you're doing.* Politely acknowledge their desire to help, but be just as strong in asserting your capability to handle the issue.

Solomon Says:

Meddling parents don't realize they are know-it-alls. If they're wrong, it costs you nothing to let them save face. Pressing them for details—questions that don't accuse or criticize— will let them expose the flaws themselves. You won't have to. If they're right, you may hear some views you can use.

THE SCRIPT

YOU. It's no secret we disagree on a lot of matters. And that's fine with me. But I think we could improve on the way we're trying to get the message across. So I'd like to play this tape for you that I recorded during dinner to let us hear how we actually sound. I realize you feel strongly about your beliefs because they have worked well for you all these years. I have no wish to change your mind and I respect your right to your opinions and ask only that you give me the same respect. We can only grow by making mistakes. I'm saying I need to make my own choices, even at the risk of failure.

GUIDELINE
When you're in the middle of a muddle, huddle.
Listen—then respectfully accept or reject and move on to something else.

53. Stop the Shame Game

Answering constant jabs that imply the fault is yours

Not only are your decisions bad, but somehow *you* are to blame for your mother's bruised feelings. Actually, she's wrong, yet you keep paying ransom to rid yourself of the guilt.

If your mother isn't punishing you verbally, she's comparing you unfavorably with your sibling. Her manipulation today triggers the anxiety and insecurity you experienced as a child.

Buried hurt feelings surface as you recall her saying: "I'm going to have a heart attack if you keep that up." "What will the neighbors say?" "Why can't you make better grades like your sister?" "How can I love you when you do such things?"

Now that you're older, you realize you were never allowed to let off steam and release your hostile feelings. Your mother then, and now, is determined to keep control by replenishing the reasons for you to feel guilty.

THE GOAL
Stop the emotional blackmail.

THE PLAN
1. *Set the alarm.* When you hear the "after all I did for you" signal, a bell should sound in your brain. It's time to accept responsibility for your own well-being by stopping the charge instantly.

2. *Try a humorous retort.* Imply that you know that she knows that she's still trying to dominate your life, but you're laughing with her, not at her.

3. *Switch to discussing your mother's needs.* Instead of getting mad and defending your actions, be generous and humor her.

4. *Refuse to accept a sibling comparison.* Let your mother know you simply won't discuss such a ridiculous statement.

THE SCRIPT

MOM. How could someone so smart do such a stupid thing?

YOU. [*laughing it off*]. We geniuses are born to be misunder-stood.

MOM. If you really cared about me, you'd come over more often. Can't you see how I'm suffering?

YOU. Yes, is there something I can get you now?

MOM. Why can't you be more like your sister?

YOU. You must be feeling at loose ends to say that. You know I can't be Gina. We're two different people. That's like comparing apples and oranges.

MOM. [*persisting*]. But Gina is considerate, while you are—

YOU. [*interrupting*]. I've asked you hundreds of times to stop comparing us. Since you won't stop, I don't intend to discuss that anymore.

GUIDELINE
Divert, don't defend—just shove aside the guilt that parents heap.
Shift the discussion from your actions to your parent's problems.

54. Your Name-Calling Isn't Doing Anyone Any Good

Confronting hurtful name-calling and doomsday predictions

Some parents go beyond exaggerating your mistakes. They also attack with disparaging, abusive branding irons.

Now that you're grown up, how much should you blame your parents for branding you with derogatory labels during your childhood? A youngster can't escape good and bad parental influences. And it lessens feelings of guilt if you can blame current problems on parental treatment.

You grew up hearing such comments as, "You'll never amount to anything," no matter what you attempted. Every mistake was overblown. If you forgot to do something, you were an ignoramus.

Even now your mother wants to keep controlling you. You suspect she enjoys your areas of vulnerability because she doesn't want you to succeed where she failed. She seems to get her kicks picking at your confidence with statements like, "You're just like your father—a lazy loser." You're furious at your mother for marking you with an indelible brand.

THE GOAL
Slough off continuing attempts at controlling you.

THE PLAN
1. *Accept this fact: All parents make mistakes.* Most of them do the best they know how to do. If you believe your parents erred, then as a parent you will do things differently.

2. *Realize you're no longer a dependent child.* You have years of experiences and mature insight to prepare you to be responsible for how you act and for the goals you set. Your mother can't hurt you now, unless you allow her to. It's really up to you, and only you, to help yourself. Don't blame your folks for crises you yourself have created.

3. *Take the fun out of gunning you.* When your mom brandishes her branding irons, don't show you're upset. If you can convince her that you're really not bothered by what she says, she'll see, eventually, that she's wasting her breath.

4. *Try good-natured teasing.* Being kind and gentle is a totally unexpected response from you. That should leave her speechless for a few moments as it dawns on her that name-calling no longer achieves her desired outcome.

5. *Ignore the personal attack.* Either discuss the issue itself or change the subject.

Solomon Says:

When name-calling causes already knotty problems to become hopelessly entangled:

- Reduce hostility by acknowledging that your parent is upset.

- State that name-calling really doesn't resolve anything.

- Ask for a breakdown of specific charges. These you can deal with.

THE SCRIPT

MOM. There you go again. You always act before you think. You are stupid and inconsiderate and that's why you'll always be a failure.

YOU. [*smiling*]. Yes, Mom. Have you thought about putting music to that same old song? It'd make a great country ballad.

MOM. I don't understand you.

YOU. Let's just say it's possible I used bad judgment, but you also taught me to be fair [*attribute to her a quality she's proud of*] and you know deep down that using bad judgment doesn't make me a bad person.

MOM. [*reluctantly*]. I guess so.

YOU.   Now, what's really important is. . .

GUIDELINE
   Name-calling is only as destructive as you allow it to be.
   Being firm and friendly stops degradation faster than a counterattack.

55. Give Me the Benefit of the Doubt

*When parents jump to conclusions
without waiting for facts*

Your folks don't need earplugs. They already have a closed mind. Before they interrogate you, you already are being blamed. They point their fingers before all the information is in.

It's tough enough to abate anger when you *did* do something wrong, but it's even tougher to defend yourself at the same time. In the beginning, you go mute, stunned by the unfair attack.

It seems you can't do anything right. Whatever goes wrong, your parents assume you're responsible. You'd be glad to accept the blame and apologize if you were at fault. But you're not. Your problem is dealing with their suspicions. Their wrath stems from unfounded accusations, incomplete information, and erroneous conclusions.

But they are so angry, they can't hear your explanation. You all end up hurling irrelevant nasty cracks. The initial charge which started the ruckus is long forgotten. Though you regret losing your cool, you're so provoked that you can't talk to them without fighting. Tune in tomorrow for the next episode.

THE GOAL
Shift the rage from each other to the issue.

THE PLAN
1. *Stay put.* Don't angrily respond, deny, or walk away. Let them vent and calm down before you try to respond. You can't get through to people who are emotionally high or low.

2. *Remain calm without counteraccusing.* This is a chance to turn things around.

3. *Make them earn their right to be wrong.* Move the discussion to the facts of the case. Ask for their help with sorting out the problem and examining the evidence. Seek agreement on the exact facts, based on available information.

4. *Answer the issues one at a time.* Offer to find out any essential missing data and ask them to withhold judgment until you get back to them.

THE SCRIPT

DAD. How could someone with your brains and background be such an idiot? I am so disappointed. You, of all people, to do this.

YOU. I know you're upset, but when you attack me it's hard to talk to you. Can we discuss this calmly and reasonably?

DAD. I am being reasonable. What you did was stupid!

YOU. Look, Dad, you have a right to criticize my action, but there's no reason for the cruel words and harsh treatment even if you are correct in your assumptions.

DAD. [*winding down*]. OK, let's look at what you did.

YOU. Yes, please, let's examine what you think I did and give me a chance to explain the situation. If I did do something wrong, I know it's my responsibility to make it right. But if I didn't, don't you think there's a possibility I can prove that as well?

GUIDELINE

When you're being blamed, first gather and review the facts.

Though tempting, don't strike back when you're unjustly accused. If it turns out the error was yours, don't overapologize or you'll make the fault seem worse than it actually is.

56. Why Isn't Anything I Do Good Enough?

Rejecting parental affronts while
accepting their support

At times, your parents' blame game means you're walking a tightrope.

You're paying a high price for living rent free. Either you have to continue enduring insults, or you're afraid you'll have to move out. And you don't yet earn enough to make ends meet.

Because you are so dependent on this financial support, you allow your sharp-shooting parents to use you for target practice.

Everything comes under the scope of their attacks. They constantly monitor your behavior—what you eat, what time you come home, the clothes you wear, your choice of friends. You don't feel free to breathe.

You are financially stuck and emotionally drained. Because you accept their help, do they have the right to control every aspect of your life?

THE GOAL

Balance both needs—parental support and your independence. Reject the affront while you continue to accept the assistance.

THE PLAN

1. *Start saving.* Sacrifice one activity a week, if necessary, to find money to put away. It's well worth it no matter how little the actual amount. Carrying out your plan will help you feel you are in control of your life and on the road to freedom.

2. *Be more assertive.* Initiate discussion of the problem. If you don't speak up now, you'll feel victimized forevermore.

3. *Agree on commonsense rules.* Listening to your parents' concerns and coming across as willing to adhere to mutually acceptable regulations will give you new respect and you'll feel yourself on a higher footing.

Insults that are put into motion spin around with centrifugal force, and they don't stop until something intervenes. That something is a polite and firm refusal to accept any more rude treatment or to return any more barbs. Acknowledge that parents deserve to be honored, and state that you also deserve to be treated with respect. If you sense hostility is behind the rudeness, bring it out in the open to discuss and resolve the difficulties.

THE SCRIPT

YOU. I have some good news. I'm being considered for an interviewer's job with a placement company that—

MOM. This is what we sent you to college for!

YOU. Mom and Dad, can we talk? It seems to me that whatever I try is never good enough. What is it that you want me to do that I'm not doing?

MOM. We'd like to know that you'll stop drifting and get some direction in your life.

YOU. I do have a plan. I'm working toward a managerial position. This company has a good policy for helping its people stay on a career track. What else?

DAD. You come home at all hours. You know how your mother worries. And when she can't sleep, she keeps me up, too.

YOU. Okay, if that's a big problem, I'll tell you when I expect to be home. If I'm going to be later, I'll call you. What else do you think would ease the tension around here?

GUIDELINE
Don't sit and stew—do.

When you're stuck on the horns of a dilemma, look for additional possibilities. Find a new way to go through the horns.

57. Please Respect My Time

Handling unreasonable demands made on your free time

Another ploy is to make you feel guilty for not constantly being on call.

It's like trying to keep a bowl full when the water runs out of a large hole in the bottom. No matter how hard you try, it's not enough. No matter how much time you spend with your mother, she always wants much more. And you don't have the extra hours to give her. You're already pressured by so many demands that when she twists the vise a little tighter, you scream for mercy.

Besides handling your executive position, you have responsibilities to your husband and children. You used to pride yourself on your ability to manage your time, but this situation is impossible. You've sacrificed doing anything for your own pleasure. Now there's nothing left to cut out.

One of her special tricks is to magnify a minor problem as a major crisis so that you'll drop everything and rush over. By unreasonably forcing her will on you, you realize she's taking advantage of your love and manipulating you with guilt feelings. Although you're an only child devoted to Mom, you know you can't go on like this.

THE GOAL
Say no without guilt.

THE PLAN
1. *Face reality.* Your mother's desire to monopolize you is insatiable. It wouldn't matter how many more hours you give her, she won't be happy until you're under her wing twenty-four hours a day. So get off the merry-go-round right now.

2. *Set a reasonable limit.* After refiguring and balancing the priorities from the rest of your life, you decide the amount of time you can spare to visit your mother. Announce this decision to her.

3. *Arrange alternatives.* Depending on her condition, plan for her to attend outside events, organize visits with old friends, hire a companion. You'll be meeting her need for attention and sociability in a far better way as well as getting your own life back.

THE SCRIPT

MOM. Frances, what took you so long to get here? I thought you knew how badly I needed that heating pad.

YOU. Mom, we need to get a few things straightened out. I know how proud you were when I was promoted to vice president of my company. And I know you want me to be as good a mother to Beverly and Bill as you've been to me.

MOM. Of course, what are you getting at?

YOU. Time. Or rather, the limitations on my time. I have many responsibilities and many things I want to do, such as visit more with you. But I can't do everything you and I would like.

MOM. You're not going to stop coming here, are you?

YOU. Naturally, I'll be here. But because I can't come as often, I've arranged for some changes that I know will make you happy. . .

GUIDELINE

Stop and refuel—you're running on empty.
You won't have anything left to give unless you start taking care of yourself. Begin saying no to preserve the relationship.

58. I Just Want What's Best for You

When the more you do for older parents, the worse it gets

Have you stopped to consider that giving too much of yourself can be harmful to both of you? It's extremely difficult for people who have been independent all their lives to ask for and accept help.

While you mean well, when you try to do some extra things for your dad, instead of being grateful he gets resentful and unhappy.

You love Dad, and you want his later years to be as good and safe as possible. With your mother gone and with his diminished eyesight, you're afraid that he can no longer take care of himself adequately. Since he retired, he's alone a lot. When you suggested that a nursing home might be a solution, this infuriated him. He accused you of robbing him of self-respect.

THE GOAL
Minimize stress by salvaging your parent's dignity.

THE PLAN
1. *Recognize the uniqueness of each older person.* While many may share certain situations, for example, less chance to mingle or such common chronic health conditions as decreased vision, they have different backgrounds and experiences. What aids some distresses others.

2. *Let your parent do for himself as much as possible.* This isn't the first time he's had to adjust to new circumstances. He adjusted to retirement and to your mother's death. Now give him a chance to adjust to his physical problem as well.

3. *Look for new ways for your dad to be able to do more.* Perhaps you can make physical changes in the home to eliminate some safety hazards. Go through the house together to spot the potential problems and decide how to handle them.

4. *Investigate community social and emotional assistance.* He might like to be transported to a daytime adult center where he could make friends, enjoy activities, and be encouraged to do as much as he can.

THE SCRIPT

DAD. Quit reminding me of the shape I'm in. I don't need your pity. I get along OK. I enjoy listening to music. I enjoy going for walks. I'm doing all right, so stop nagging me.

YOU. Well, I'm sorry, I didn't mean to upset you. I love you and maybe I've been worrying unnecessarily.

DAD. At last. I got through to you.

YOU. However, I think there are a few things we can do around the apartment to make living here a bit more comfortable. For example, if we moved the sofa over here, that would give you a lot more room to walk around. What do you think?

DAD. OK, OK, I guess that would work.

YOU. Since you don't drive anymore, I checked into a senior center a few miles from here. They provide transportation and have all sorts of activities. If you'd be willing to give it a try, I promise I'll stop nagging you.

Guideline

Help the aging remain in the mainstream by providing links to the outside world.

Isolation is a chief cause of stress and anxiety among the elderly. Look for opportunities to change the routine.

Chapter XI

Teenagers

We all make mistakes, so stop kicking yourself. Most teens know if their folks are trying and mean well, and they realize you have problems, too. While you might be your child's most important influence, you're not totally to blame when things don't go right. Many other factors contribute to behavior and personality.

However, it is vital that you *use* the adult authority you have to instruct your kids. No bribing, coaxing, delaying. They are to do what's expected. Otherwise, your teens do the disciplining and you bring up a bunch of barbarians.

It's a foregone conclusion that teens can manipulate you, but this chapter concentrates on your being helpful without being manipulative. This is a time of struggling for teens. You need ways to encourage them to express their problems, identify the desired outcome, and come up with a plan of action. They never outgrow the need for your assurance and pats on the back. Your helping hand doesn't make them more dependent; it frees them to grow.

And as for their questionable tastes and habits, have faith. They will improve—eventually—without your comments. Show your love by setting reasonable limits, a balance between your comfort and their freedom.

See also Chapter 84, "More Tips for Talking to Teens."

59. Let's Be Certain
We Understand Each Other

*When your kids
won't play by your rules*

Before we discuss this situation, let's get something straight. Frankly, some matters you parents assume are your problems really belong to your kids. You'll automatically rid yourself of a lot of headaches if you'll shut up about how they dress or wear their hair or talk on the phone or clean up their room. Choose your battles—you can't fight on every front or you won't be heard at all.

• • •

Now about your teen, Dulce. Some of your fights with her stem from your strong sense of responsibility. You say it's the role of parents to control every aspect of your daughter's behavior and if you say "you should" often enough, she'll change. She hasn't.

You're at your wit's end. Dulce, you claim, must have a disobedience device built into her personality development.

Nevertheless, on the really important issues—her health, safety, and future—you know you must get through to her. You have to be able to discuss such matters as rude behavior, taking drugs, driving drunk, teenage pregnancy, or taking money without permission.

But how can you make her aware of dangers if she won't listen?

THE GOAL

Teach self-control with effective ways to cope.

THE PLAN

1. *Reduce and reword your instructions.* Keep clear, crisp, and concise rules on what's desirable and allowable. Unless she wants to do something illegal or immoral, give her the choice to obey or disobey.

Just make sure the consequences are perfectly clear: She'll pay if she doesn't obey.

2. *Be consistent with enforcement.* This can't be an empty warning. Follow through as promised. And no bribing to get compliance! Also don't tease with "we'll see" when you know you'll refuse later.

3. *Let your praise stand alone.* Don't ruin it with stored-up criticism or comparing what's good this time to past mistakes.

4. *Judge the action, not the person.* Accepting your teen in a genuinely friendly way lets you reject the behavior while still supporting her. Punishment for wrongdoing is because she broke the rule, not because she is a bad person.

5. *Show your own confidence.* Nagging ("As long as *we* pay the bills, you'd better shape up!") doesn't penetrate; it just irritates. Let her express her anger, without your playing the martyr. If you complain and then do her assigned task for her, she learns it's okay to take advantage. Be matter-of-fact with her ultimatums. Don't buckle in a panic when she threatens you if she can't have her way.

6. *Teach your teen how to deal with problems.* People who abuse drugs and alcohol don't have more effective ways to cope. You're not after blind obedience, but building self-confidence, self-control, and respect. She sees things differently than you do. She needs a little time to think things out. Give it to her. Then impose a deadline to comply and enforce it. When she threatens to leave, calmly extract from her a statement of the problem and the hoped-for result. Don't argue with her conclusions—simply shift the focus to realistic aspects. Give her room to correct herself.

7. *Talk to parents of your teen's friends.* Aim for a common acceptable standard of behavior. Rules will be easier to enforce if, for example, curfews are similar. If not, then stick to what's best for your teen.

THE SCRIPT

MOM. *[inconvenienced by her thoughtlessness].* I was late for work this morning because I had to stop and get gas. You didn't refill the tank last night as you promised to do whenever I let you use the car.

DULCE. I'm sorry, Mom, I forgot.

MOM. That's not good enough, Dulce. We have to figure out

another arrangement right now. The choice is up to you—follow the rule and you'll be allowed to use my car at night; break the rule for any reason, and you won't. What would you say would be a fair consequence? [*Agree on a precise rule and enforce it.*]

Solomon Says:

Teach your kids ways to control outbursts:

- If it's a cry to get attention, set aside a daily half-hour for fun, playing with them—games, sports ... whatever works.

- Explain flexibility when things don't go their way. Ask, "What else could you do?"

- Discuss their concern about not fitting in. Together, explore ways to overcome this.

• • •

DAD.   Dulce, we realize nobody likes being bugged. So your mom and I promise we won't be pestering you anymore about your overcharging on our account at the mall. But let's be certain we understand each other. As we previously decided, if we have to pay anything above our agreed amount, there won't be any evening socializing for you until you've paid off that bill.

DULCE. You're always picking on me. Everything I do is wrong. As soon as I get a little saved up, I'm outta here.

DAD.   You're obviously upset. Is there something else bothering you? Sometimes it helps just to look at the problem in a new way. What seems to be the trouble? Maybe we can help.

• • •

MOM.   Dulce, I was putting your laundry in your drawer and I found this. Your dad and I want to talk to you about it and make sure you understand the seriousness of using drugs. We're very concerned about how involved you are. But even though we're very upset over the way you've endangered yourself, we want you to know that we love you and want to help you. So explain to us what's been happening and together we'll figure out some appropriate action.

GUIDELINE
  Teens want independence but need your help in learning to handle it.

60. I Hear You and I Want to Help

When they need to learn how to handle painful experiences

When your child is hurting, you want to make the situation better. Sometimes your actions make it worse.

Josh acts out his rage and frustrations. A couple of his former friends have become part of the in-group at school. This crowd doesn't like Josh, so his alleged friends have written him off, too. Cliques can be cruel, inflicting pain on those they exclude. Naturally Josh is hurt and feels inadequate. His self-esteem has plummeted.

In Josh's mind, if he could start wearing clothes with the right labels, he might be accepted. Advertisers certainly have bombarded him with that message. So you gave in and bought him the expensive clothes. When that didn't help him belong, Josh was hurt even more. He's so angry now, he's vowing to get even.

On the one hand, you know the kids he wants to be with have superficial values. Their confidence depends on their possessions, which are more important to them than any real values such as being a caring or ethical person. But on the other hand, you know how badly Josh wants to belong and you don't know what else to do to help him be accepted.

THE GOAL

Help your teen develop a healthy acceptance of himself.

He needs the self-confidence that comes from regarding himself as a worthy human being. Trying to get him into a group with superficial values defeats that aim.

THE PLAN

1. *Encourage constructive ways to express himself and deal with harsh experiences.* First, allow him to let off steam. He's feeling bad enough, don't pounce.

- *Concentrate on good conversations.* Draw out his thinking. Listen with respect and interest, rather than giving him answers. He has to know you take his concerns seriously. Shift the talk away from pinpointing blame toward planning (with, not for, him) to get what he wants. Respect his desire to be emancipated. Some thoughts he considers none of your business (e.g., hair, clothes, room, music) so don't invade his privacy.

- *Point up the need to be open-minded.* In order to meet new people, we all have to take a risk and go up and talk to others. That's often the way we find a good friend.

- *Help him develop a potential talent or interest.* In addition to sports and school clubs for making new friends, painting, music, dancing, acting, writing, chorus, and band are especially motivating if there's a public production or exhibit. Or he may want to learn a new subject or skill such as computer programming or video production.

2. *Help him separate what's important from what isn't.* You can assist him in thinking things through by asking pointed questions to sharpen the focus. Get him to state the problem and the desired result (for example, how to get acceptance and recognition because it's earned and deserved). Then discuss ways to bring this about.

3. *Help him believe in himself.* He needs to feel he's good at something so encourage activities in which he can succeed. Talk about his strengths. Praise every achievement even if it doesn't meet your expectation. A perfectionist parent can destroy a child's self-esteem.

4. *Support him with frequent feedback.* Be kind and understanding as you define his limits. Keep him on an even keel by praising what he does well along with discussing how to correct his poor reactions. He's learning to handle peer pressure and needs encouragement to speak his mind and resist being pushed around. Temper your own emotions—get over your own anger before talking so that you can help him deal with the actual problem. He needs your support at home to overcome challenges and defeats at school and with friends.

THE SCRIPT

JOSH. Some friends they turned out to be! I'll show them. I'll figure out a good way to get even. [*Don't interrupt. Let him vent.*]

YOU. I can only imagine how disappointed you must be.

JOSH. I thought I could trust them and they turned on me.

YOU. What was it you expected them to do?

JOSH. Help me belong to the in-group, of course.

YOU. If you did belong, what would that do for you?

JOSH. You gotta be kidding. If I belonged, I'd be accepted and recognized.

YOU. So what you really want is to be accepted and recognized, right? Why don't we talk about some other ways you might get good recognition. You have a great flare for cartooning. Have you thought about getting on the school newspaper staff?

JOSH. You really think my work is good enough?

YOU. Absolutely. It's certainly worth a try.

JOSH. Do you think the kids would accept me then?

Solomon Says:

Some important ways to give help:

- Break up the problem into manageable pieces. Put it into words that your kids use.

- Teach brainstorming. When they can come up with many possible solutions, your teens feel in control. Remember, the far-fetched often ignites the feasible.

- Tell kids it's OK to ask for help. We all have to do this after we've tried and can't fix a problem. When frustration reaches a high-enough level, people become desperate, even violent.

YOU. Yes, that's honest recognition. You know, Josh, the kids like you because of who you are, not because of things you possess. They like you when you share your talent with them and it makes you feel good inside. Whenever you give something of yourself to others, you feel proud of yourself and we feel very proud of you.

GUIDELINE
Helping build self-esteem diminishes anger and frustration.

61. Your Walking Away Won't Solve Anything

When "I don't want to talk about it" ends the discussion

Conversations turn into monologues. You can't pry a response out of your teen.

Your communicating skills are really put to the test. You're trying to reach your teen so that he'll open up to you. But Art seems deliberate in wanting to unnerve you. He looks right through you with that evil-eye stare, not saying a word.

If you complain, he enjoys watching you blow up. And if you try rephrasing what he says to you, that infuriates him.

Any small matter can quickly become a full-blown power struggle. You're so tired of the arguments and the escalation. And nothing you say gets through.

THE GOAL

Tune into the same channel for reasonable conversations.

THE PLAN

1. *Think about what your child is probably going through.* How would you feel in that situation? Angry, hurt, disappointed, manipulated? Empathize. Show you're trying to understand.

2. *Give an angry teen time to vent.* You can afford to be generous and be the sponge to sop up the hurt.

3. *Control your own fury.* Keep it positive. Your child will always be facing difficult situations so you want to teach him how to cope with problems. Check your negative emotions before you speak. Resolve problems by offering help, not scorn. You can hate the behavior, but love the child. When praise is deserved, say it. Let your teen's thinking be part of forming and carrying out a plan.

4. *Be nonjudgmental, taking what he says seriously.* He wants you to see the situation from his—not your—point of view. Listen to him with an interest to learn rather than to judge. Your teen wants your approval but may not be sure how you'll react. Therefore, he may withhold his thoughts to avoid a fight or lying to you.

5. *Allow your teen to keep some thoughts to himself.* Help him with problem-solving skills; but if you press him for details about his friends and activities, he'll feel you're unreasonable in mistrusting his judgment. He wants some part of his life to remain private. He thinks you can't possibly understand his desire to fit in and to be independent, so he'd rather talk to his friends. Let him take responsibility for issues that concern him and him alone. Stay out of it and you'll all be happier. He'll make mistakes, but that's how he'll learn.

6. *Plan for family discussions.* Use the dinner hour for conversations instead of eating in front of the TV.

Solomon Says:

To get teens to share their thoughts:

- DO create an accepting, mutually trusting atmosphere. They have to know you'll listen to their side and that you try to understand their feelings.

- DON'T jump all over them with sarcastic, instant "you shoulda" lectures.

- DON'T pry for details you don't need to know. Respect their loyalty to friends. When they trust you, it won't be snitching—but helping—to discuss a friend heading for deep trouble.

THE SCRIPT

MOM.   Hi, you look like you had a rough day. What happened in school?

ART.   Must you question everything I do!

MOM.   I can see you're really angry right now. Maybe you'd care to tell me what happened, even if I'm not able to

	help you. Would you like to talk about it? Perhaps together we can figure out what to do.
ART.	As if you really care what I think.
MOM.	I do care. Try me out, I'm listening.
ART.	I think I may have failed my chemistry test. It was really, really tough. All the kids were complaining about it afterwards.
MOM.	That's encouraging. If everyone else found it difficult, your teacher will probably curve the grades because she doesn't want to have a whole class that failed.
ART.	I hadn't thought about it that way. Jimmy and Donna said they studied for four hours last night.
MOM.	What would happen if four or five of you got together for a weekly study session? Do you think you could help each other?
ART.	Maybe. I'll think about it.
MOM.	I know you studied hard for that test and I'm proud of the effort you made. Maybe this isn't as bad as you fear. What do you think?
ART.	OK, I feel a little better now. I think the study group might work. I'll try out the idea on the others. Thanks, Mom.

GUIDELINE

Don't impose your solutions—let the choice come from your teen.

62. This Is Your Responsibility—
   Don't Make It Ours

*Gaining cooperation instead
of doing their chores*

Many teens who agree to your rules have their own timetable. And that drives you up the wall.

It's simple enough. One of June's duties is to clear the table and put the dishes in the dishwasher. The phone rings and she gets tied up in an hour-long chat while the dishes sit waiting for her. You wait patiently and don't say anything, but you're fuming inside. You suspect she's either trying to get you to do her work or defeat you in this skirmish.

While you're waiting, one of your friends drops by. You're embarrassed that at 8:00 P.M. there's a table full of dirty dishes. When the friend leaves, you and your teen come to blows.

June can't understand why you're so upset, claiming she fully intended to fulfill her chores. Apparently, part of asserting her independence is not doing whatever you want done too soon. So she dawdles and keeps delaying in order to save face. You finally realize that she's the one setting the pace and dictating terms. And all your fussing and fuming isn't changing the pattern.

THE GOAL
Set rules your teen will adhere to.

THE PLAN
1. *Issue a clear statement of your expectations.* Calmly show confidence and respect while explaining what you intend to do about a situation that's making you miserable. Come across as fair, giving equal weight to your need for a neat home and her need to socialize with her friends.

2. *Ask for suggestions on meeting both your needs.* It may be a minor issue, but it's a good opportunity to teach problem-solving skills.

3. *Explain what action will be taken.* No more fights about the dishes vs. the telephone. No more delaying tactics. These are the new rules that will accommodate both of you. If she chooses not to abide, she understands the consequences.

Solomon Says:

Do you realize...

... Your kids are laughing at you because you're such an easy mark? What's more, you're not helping. You're always the crutch, so how can they learn to stand alone? And don't kid yourself, when you build up a head of steam, your suppressed anger comes through. Deal with it. Show concern, make suggestions—but it's their problem to work out.

THE SCRIPT

YOU.   We need a better agreement on handling the dinner dishes. I find it terribly embarrassing when people drop by and the dirty dishes are still on the table. I appreciate your need to talk to your friends, and I'm sure you can understand my need to have a tidy home. What do you think we can do to meet both our needs?

JUNE.   Mom, the problem is that's the only time when my friends and I can talk on the phone.

YOU.   OK, then let's figure out a way to speed things up. From now on, I will make sure all the food is put away while you clear and stack the dishwasher. OK?

JUNE.   That would help, but what if the phone rings?

YOU.   I can see how important those talks are to you, June. But it won't take you that long to finish. If the phone rings, I'll take your messages and say you'll call back in a few minutes.

JUNE.   Aw, Mom.

YOU.   Now it's up to you, June. That's the way it's going to be.

Either you go by our agreement, which is fair to both of us, or you won't be having any telephone communication at night. The choice is yours.

GUIDELINE

Most delaying tactics can be negotiated.

To negotiate you have to hear the other's need. Nagging prolongs procrastination; showing confidence accelerates action. You help most by not doing for others what they're able to and should do for themselves.

63. I Didn't Raise You in a Barn

When their mess makes a trail throughout the house

It's bad enough your kid's room is a wreck. Must your whole house look like a jungle too?

You and your wife are tired when you come home from work. The first thing you see is a weaving line that starts just inside the front door. Jacket, shoes, books, and whatever else your teen decided to shed the moment he walked in.

You get so angry that you lose your temper. You start screaming at him and calling him a slob who ought to live in a pig sty. That gets you nowhere.

The next day the place is as bad as before. You've tried leaving it. Your wife eventually picks up his things herself, which only encourages Rick's bad habit.

You know you shouldn't be name-calling, but it doesn't seem to matter. Whatever you do, he has no incentive to try to improve, and you and your wife are at your wit's end.

THE GOAL

Place responsibility where it belongs.

THE PLAN

1. *Negotiate a deal.* You promise to stop nagging him about cleaning up his room and he promises to stop dumping all his stuff every place except his own room.

2. *Attach a penalty clause to the agreement.* Together, agree on a fair and reasonable punishment if you find any of his belongings strewn in the living or dining areas.

3. *Make it easy to comply.* Furnish him with a coat rack, a place for his books, a tray for his keys and wallet, or whatever else might encourage the behavior you want.

4. *Set a deadline*. Establishing limits is fair because everyone knows what to expect and what will happen, by when, if the agreement is not carried out.

THE SCRIPT

DAD.   OK, Rick, let's see what we can work out. You must be sick of us yelling at you repeatedly to pick up your stuff.

RICK.   You got that right.

DAD.   Then let's make a deal. We promise to stop if you promise to pick up.

RICK.   Sure, sure, that's cool.

MOM.   There's a little more to this deal, Rick. We're confident that you mean to pick up after yourself, but in this case you're going to have to make a decision. Either you keep all your things in your room, as you agreed, or there'll be a penalty.

RICK.   What kind of penalty?

MOM.   If you hold up your end of the deal, then we know you can keep a promise and act responsibly. You will continue being allowed use of the car. If you are irresponsible, that privilege will be taken away and you'll need to find other transportation. No more nagging from us and no more excuses from you. Are we all in agreement?

GUIDELINE

Put the burden on the right back—don't assume another's responsibilities.

Chapter XII

In-Laws and Other Relatives

What a conglomeration! Your sisters, brothers, aunts and uncles, cousins, in-laws—every relative knows better than you how you should run your life.

Some people have the idea that it's okay to treat relatives differently from the way they treat others. They might be terribly polite to friends and colleagues, but they feel perfectly free to poke around in the private lives of their kin. Not just being nosy, but meddling and interfering. They may graciously accept a faux pas committed by a friend, but they'll bite the head off a sibling who does the same thing.

Where is it written that those born into your family, or joined through marriage, have the right to insinuate themselves into your decisions? And then, if you don't conform to their way of thinking, they feel they not only have this right, but also a duty, to set you straight.

Sometimes they act out of jealousy, or they still hold a grudge because they felt you insulted them thirteen years ago. Others are simply haughty enough to think they have all the answers.

Chapter XII offers ways to keep the peace while gaining peace of mind.

64. This Is Really No Concern of Yours

Politely telling meddlers to mind their own business

So far you've remained outwardly calm. But you'd really like to anoint Cousin Lucy's head with your cup of tea as your controlled rage runneth over.

Where does she get the nerve to ask you all sorts of personal questions that have absolutely no bearing on her own life? What reason is there for her to know your salary, why you went to the doctor last week, or the details of a spat you had recently with your father?

Not content with prying, she injects additional irritants with her unasked-for advice. She sticks her nose into what you ought to do. Sometimes Lucy is a retro advisor, sermonizing on what you should have done, as if that does any good after the fact. Her advice costs nothing and that's what it's worth. But her attitude is that if she doesn't say how she feels, how will you know she cares about you? That kind of caring you can live without.

THE GOAL

Reestablish your right to run your own life.

THE PLAN

1. *Cut her off at the pass.* The next time she tries to invade your privacy, let her know your personal information is off-limits to others not affected by it. You know what's coming, so practice a few prepared responses.

2. *Stay poised and gracious.* Smile politely as you reject her brand of help.

3. *Watch her run to find another target.* When her snooping and interfering boomerang, you deny her the satisfaction she was getting from trying to control you.

Dealing with the dilemma of role reversal in meddling:

Although you resent being the "butt-ee," at times you ask yourself: Should I become the "butt-er"? Here's a guideline. If the health or safety of another is endangered, yes; otherwise, back off.

THE SCRIPT

LUCY. I hear you got a raise last week. So how much are you making now?

YOU. Really, Lucy, I'm sure you didn't realize when you asked me, that that's a very private matter. Now tell me, what's interesting in your life?

• • •

LUCY. You know you really should tell Albert that he's ruining his reputation by—

YOU. Oh, thank you, Lucy, but I've already taken care of it.

• • •

LUCY. I know you're smart enough to figure this out for yourself, but [*implying you're really inept and need her help*] if I were you, I'd tell your boss—

YOU. [*smiling while interrupting*]. Lucy, I know you tell me these things out of your concern for me. But let me assure you, I'm fine and really quite capable of running my own life.

GUIDELINE

Don't lock horns with meddlers—toot your own horn instead and lock onto your self-confidence.

65. Your Smugness Is a Real Pain

*Coping with
know-it-alls*

Here come the relatives who not only know all the answers but also feel obliged to force-feed them to you at every opportunity.

Your older brother Marty is painfully arrogant. Abundantly opinionated, he's convinced that only he can see the correct path to take. You, according to him, just stumble along. He's right; you're wrong. Period. If something goes awry, it's because you were incompetent applying his advice.

You're worn out from his dogmatic lectures and superiority attitude. You've tried to get him to see things as you do, but his mind is closed and locked up tight. No new thoughts are allowed to penetrate. You often find yourself going along with him because, although you resent it, that's less exhausting than trying to debate an issue.

How can you stand up to such an overwhelming torrent?

THE GOAL

Get your brother to quit bugging you.

THE PLAN

1. *Recite a mantra to stay calm.* Repeat to yourself over and over a predetermined phrase, such as, "If I stay cool, I win."

2. *Act befuddled.* Pretend to be at a loss rather than counterargue. People like Marty become more persistent when challenged. Keep asking questions that require specific answers and listen attentively. Continue pressing for details and restating what you've heard to show you understood.

3. *Reconsider your view as you review the facts.* Is there merit to what he says? Perhaps some middle ground would be good? Or are you convinced now that you had the right solution all along? If so, organize your data so that you can make an accurate, positive argument.

4. *Strongly affirm your position.* Staunchly assert your facts in a concise, unemotional manner, and then stop discussing it any more. Smile and, if necessary, walk away. It is your decision to accept or reject. In that way, you are in control.

Solomon Says:

When facing know-it-alls:

- DON'T argue. These self-proclaimed experts on all matters are so convinced they're right, any other opinion (like yours) has to be wrong. If you debate, you won't stand a chance under the avalanche of their of-course-I'm-right "facts."

- DO acknowledge their position. You needn't argue, but you don't want a family feud.

- DO state your case when you're ready and then end the talk. You can't change them, but you can control the length of the conversation and the fury you feel.

THE SCRIPT

MARTY.   I don't care what you say. You've got an obligation you have to honor.

YOU.   [*don't argue, ask*]. How long do you think we'd have to continue staying with Mom? How can my wife and I uproot our lives? Why are you so sure Mom would agree?

MARTY.   I would estimate about three months. Tell Mary this will be temporary, just until Mom gets back on her feet. Mom won't want to disrupt your life, but she knows we can't afford a live-in helper.

YOU.   You may be right, but it seems to me there are a few other options we can consider.

MARTY.   No, we've ruled out her staying alone and—

YOU.   [*interrupting*]. Hold on. Yes, I have to honor my obligation, but don't you also have to do more than help out with money? I understand that you have to travel a lot, but we both have to share in Mom's care. So I've decided to have Mom stay at my home when you're away. When you're back in town, it will be your turn.

MARTY. [*caught off guard*]. Well. . .maybe that could work.

YOU. [*changing the subject*]. Tell me, how's your tennis game coming along? [*Act as though the matter has been settled—your way.*]

GUIDELINE

Without challenging opinions, expose the sermonizer to your views.

66. Let's Accept It— You're You; I'm Me

What to say when you're the target of sibling rivalry

You should be used to your brother's jealousy by now. Whatever you have, your older sibling Paul covets—your job, your recognition, your money, your clothes, even your girlfriend.

It's been that way ever since you were kids. He was angry because you were a straight-A student. In high school, you made the football team and he didn't. Every time something good happened to you, he felt deflated and lost more self-esteem.

Now the worst part is the nasty things Paul says and does to put you in a bad light, especially with the rest of the family. As Aesop observed, those who can't reach the grapes claim they are sour. Paul lies to you or about you. He resurrects what should remain buried just to stack his attacks with irrelevant incidents.

Paul tries to get your goat, to goad you into exploding, apparently to shake your self-confidence and control. Nevertheless, you want to improve the relationship but don't know how to start.

THE GOAL
End the antagonism and become friends.

THE PLAN
1. *Take the risk and break the ice.* Arrange a quiet meeting in neutral territory. Assume a little of the blame. Maybe you did (and do) flout your successes. If you're guilty, say you'll try harder to correct the habit.

2. *Explain your need for his approval and friendship.* He can't read tea leaves—tell him you want to be friends. Recount how, over the years, you've tried desperately to get his attention and recognition. But the more you tried, the worse the relationship became.

3. *Be generous.* Encourage him with admiration of his good qualities. Help build up his self-esteem to reduce his need to tear you down.

4. *Substitute lighthearted banter for reprimands.* Let him know in a friendly way that his lies and nasty remarks really hurt, but you'd like all that to be in the past.

THE SCRIPT

YOU. We need to talk and it's long overdue. We've been at each other's throats for years. I think it started when I got higher grades and I guess I rubbed your nose in it. For all those times I've been a pompous fool, I do apologize.

PAUL. Well, I never thought you'd ever admit to that.

YOU. What you didn't realize is that you were my older brother and you never wanted anything to do with me. And all I longed for was your approval. But the more I achieved, the more you resented it.

PAUL. There was no way I could compete with you. It was demoralizing.

YOU. But Paul, there was so much about you that I did and do admire. I wish I had your musical talent. And your sense of humor. And I've become a bit pudgy, but you're in great shape. You should be feeling pretty good about yourself.

PAUL. That's easy for you to say.

YOU. Well, it's true, and I really hope we can put our hurts aside and be friends. Only promise me, Pinocchio, no more lies about me or your nose will grow longer!

GUIDELINE

It takes two to tangle—accept part of the blame.

If you're sincere in wanting to end sibling rivalry, reach out and admit your own shortcomings.

67. At Least Our Dog Likes Us

When whatever you do,
you can't please your in-laws

You've already struck out. Is there any point to keep trying?

Your wife's parents drive you to distraction. They've never really accepted your ability to make good decisions even though you run a successful business. Cynthia and her folks were very close. After she married you, they couldn't let go.

They're still overly involved; they act as though you and Cynthia are incapable of existing without their incessant input.

And no matter what you do, it's never quite good enough for them. Not out and out criticism, but uncomfortable, veiled sarcasm. They don't like your friends. You don't bring their grandchild over often enough. You should have bought a safer car. Ad infinitum.

The advice is constant and demeaning—as if you don't have the brains to drive slowly when the streets are wet. Your wife seems unaware of the problem. Cynthia continues a loving relationship with your in-laws while you feel shut out of their tight little clan.

THE GOAL
Present a solid front to overcome the affronts.
Eventually, you'd like to be accepted as part of the family.

THE PLAN
1. *Talk to your wife.* This is a discussion you should have had long ago. Your feelings have been building until the constant migraine is interfering with your daily life. You can do something about this situation. Your mate might not even be aware of your perceptions.

2. *Aim for a team approach.* Explain to your wife how in-law sarcasm and condescension make you feel. Ask for her thoughts on how best to handle the matter.

3. *Agree on a strategy.* Find one that will get her parents to ease up without antagonizing them. Your wife has to demonstrate to her parents her unequivocal support for you, refusing to hear from them anything that trivializes your feelings. The two of you must decide when and how to confer with them, whether she should pave the way for you to have your say, or if she should talk to them without you.

THE SCRIPT

CYN. I know that whatever you do and say it's because you love me and want me to be happy.

MOM. Of course, we'd do anything for you.

CYN. That's why I'm sure you aren't aware of what you're doing to Stan and me. You shower us with constant advice. Stan and I feel we're both capable of making our own decisions. If you trust us, why do you question our judgment on everything?

DAD. Cynthia, it isn't that we question your judgment. It's just that we've lived longer and want you to benefit from our experiences. All we ever wanted is what's best for you.

CYN. I know you mean well, but look at this situation from our standpoint. When you hit us constantly with unsolicited advice, I guess I'm numb to it. But your condescending tone and sarcastic remarks are really hurtful to Stan. The way you treat my husband hurts me. I'm calling this to your attention because things have to change. We can't go on this way. As much as I love you, my first loyalty is to my husband.

GUIDELINE
Back up your spouse who's being undercut by your parents.

68. Let It Go

When relatives keep digging up old, unresolved grudges

Some relatives wear the chip on their shoulder like a badge of honor.

Uncle Joe, unfortunately, deposits perceived hurts in his fail-safe memory which he stockpiles like money in the bank.

Never speaking up at the time something bothers him, Uncle Joe waits until he gets mad about something else. That activates a release button for him to bring up a totally extraneous incident. And he throws this back in your face time and time again.

You can't even remember the facts of the case, just his distorted version. You've told him repeatedly that you weren't aware of hurting his feelings, but you obviously did and for that you've apologized. When you try to show concern, he won't accept it and he won't forget his grudge or let you off the hook.

No wonder most of the family runs the other way when they see him coming.

THE GOAL
Lay to rest grudges that should have been buried long ago.

THE PLAN
1. *Put an end to apologizing.* Joe will continue to intimidate you as long as you give him the satisfaction of dragging you down. Whatever did happen is in the past and you can't change it. You said you were sorry if you inadvertently hurt him. There's nothing more to be gained by resurrecting the incident.

2. *Focus on the present.* You've already given him ample opportunities to express his resentment. Ask what he expects from you now.

3. *Smile and step back.* That gesture in itself says you are not going

to get into that subject again. If he continues to demand that you feel guilty for an alleged sin, don't bite. Shake his hand and leave.

THE SCRIPT

JOE. Don't think I've forgotten the way you insulted me by not inviting my daughter to the dinner when—

YOU. Uncle Joe, I've told you over and over that it was an oversight. I explained the circumstances to Anna and she understood.

JOE. You caused me so much hurt and embarrassment.

YOU. Uncle Joe, we've thrashed this out too many times. I've said I was sorry. What is it, exactly, that you would like me to do at this time? Where do we go from here? Are you angry about something else?

JOE. No, I'm not. But I want to make sure that you stop embarrassing your family that way.

YOU. Okay, you're right. I won't do that again. But I want you to understand that I don't intend to discuss that incident any more. Have a nice evening, Uncle Joe. Good-bye.

GUIDELINE
Snip the cord when relatives insist on tying you to the past. Don't allow past guilt to continue ad infinitum.

69. I Don't Have a Saucer of Milk

*Curbing family members
who are catty*

And how about the relatives who apparently enjoy putting you down?

What spiteful, mean, malicious things your sister-in-law has been saying to you. You hate to go to family functions when you know Judy will be there. It's always the same pattern: She comes up to you with a friendly smile, then digs her claws in.

Maybe she believes that makes her and her little family appear better than yours. You don't know what prompts her to act this way and you certainly don't want to compete with her.

You're afraid her catty remarks to other relatives will affect your relationships with the rest of the family. How can you deflect the impact?

THE GOAL

Patch the scratches and prevent future flare-ups.

THE PLAN

1. *Don't hear remarks that make you feel victimized.* When she criticizes you, don't comment. Don't show *any* reaction. Practice a mantra you can repeat to yourself during the attack ("Poor Judy needs help, poor Judy needs help, poor Judy needs help").

2. *Avoid the one-upmanship game.* When she brags about her kids or tries to compare your families, try a different tack. Be enthusiastic in your praise of the reported accomplishments of her family. You'll win her over.

3. *Keep encouraging her.* This will help defuse the anger, envy, or insecurity she may be feeling. When she realizes her catty tactics are not working, she'll stop them. Eventually you may even become good friends.

Tips to tame the cat:

- When that feline makes a beeline for your skin, don't get your dander up. The green-eyed cat is the one with the problem.

- Instead, feel the delight in rising above her remarks. Your friendliness may not change the behavior, but you'll feel awfully good about yourself. This, you do for you.

THE SCRIPT

JUDY. You're doing what? What kind of job is that for someone with your credentials?

YOU. [*Smile as though you heard a joke. Repeat the mantra to yourself. Don't say a word.*]

JUDY. Did you hear that my Lisa made the team? I'm sorry your Joan didn't.

YOU. That's great news about Lisa. I've always remarked how well coordinated she is. Takes after her mother.

JUDY. Children are such a joy, don't you think? Well, at least you have one.

YOU. Yes, they certainly are a pleasure.

JUDY. It's too bad you can't have any more children [*an assumption stated as fact*].

YOU. [*laughing*]. Oh, Judy, I don't know where you get your information. [*Smile and walk away.*]

GUIDELINE
Remove the irritating claws by gently petting the cat.

Chapter XIII

Friends

You think of friends as people you trust. Supportive. Enjoyable company. Mutual interests. But sometimes the relationship goes sour.

Instead of deriving pleasure, you feel pained. Your good friend is constantly carping on what you do wrong. Or telling you that your ideas never have merit. Or blabbing your secrets to the world. Or playing with your emotions, knowing what buttons to push to unnerve you.

Some friends enjoy playing practical jokes that truly aren't funny. Some stretch their sense of humor to cover critical comments. Others are fine when it's just the two of you, but they act up in a crude, rude manner when you are with other people.

You want the connection to be meaningful, pleasant, and positive. But sometimes you let your negative feelings go unexpressed and simmer until you finally reach the boiling point.

This chapter is about ways to restore a good friendship and if that's not possible, to get rid of hurtful "friends" when the damage from interacting is too high a price to pay.

70. I Appreciate Your Opinion, But...

When friends try to run your life

Agreed, friends should be straightforward with each other. But does that give your friend license to keep hurting your feelings and making you feel bad about yourself?

Katie knows the areas where you feel you fall short. You've complained about them often enough. She manages to seize these sensitive spots to keep putting you down. Like the time last month when you broke up with your boyfriend, and instead of helping you, her comment was, "Well, you were wrong, you should have said. . ." When you complain about her constant carping on what you do wrong, she tells you you're being silly or gets angry that you would accuse her of not caring about you.

By now you're convinced Katie's concern is shallow, like a mask covering up some unresolved feelings toward you, maybe jealousy. But she'll never admit it. The problem is that Katie can also be fun and clever and interesting. You'd like to remain friends with her, but you don't know how to make her stop her destructive routine. Or should this relationship be salvaged?

THE GOAL

Decide if the friendship is mutually honest and helpful.

THE PLAN

1. *Determine if the friendship is worth keeping.* Reevaluate what's going on. Are you just momentarily hurt or do you feel your ego has been seriously demolished? When you're with your friend, do you like or dislike yourself more?

2. *Define the negative feelings your friend brings on.* Afterwards, are you feeling frustrated, angry, afraid, inadequate, unhappy, stomped on? Do you hate yourself for not being honest about how she makes you feel?

3. *Understand you don't need your friend's approval.* It's all right for friends to disagree. You became friends because you met each other's needs. Are you still getting enough out of the friendship to make yourself take some action to preserve it?

4. *Believe you deserve respect.* Ask for it. Each of us has that right. Use your body language to back this up. Stand up straight, look her right in the eye, speak in a confident tone. Show you are dead serious and you expect to be taken seriously.

Solomon Says:

You're being belittled? Freeze!

- Stop the conversation on the spot every single time your "friends" belittle you. They need to push you down to raise their self-image, but you're nobody's pawn.

- Educate and sensitize them if you want to remain friends. ("I know you didn't realize that saying that degrades me, so knock it off.")

THE SCRIPT

KATIE. I hate to upset you, but you really blew it when you told Mark that—

YOU. [*interrupting*]. Whoa, hold it right there, Katie. I really do get upset when you keep telling me how I mess up every situation. [*You're not leveling blame; you're stating how you feel.*]

KATIE. That's part of your problem. You're too sensitive. You're just so touchy and rigid. You know you really shouldn't feel like that.

YOU. But that's how I do feel, and whether you agree with me or not, I have a right to my own feelings and a right to say how I feel.

KATIE. Are you sure that's coffee you're drinking?

YOU. Can't we talk openly and honestly without the sarcasm? I want you to be frank with me, but I can no longer tolerate the way you always put me down. When you keep telling me I use bad judgment, it doesn't help. I only hear the way that you're demeaning me and not any ideas you're saying.

KATIE. Well, I only tell you this for your own good.

YOU. No, it's not for my good. It makes me feel really bad. If you want to discuss what I can do now, I'm listening. But let's skip the negativity and sarcasm. Is it possible for you to be frank with me without cutting me up in the process?

GUIDELINE
Destroying your ego is not an act of friendship.
As the saying goes, with friends like that you don't need enemies.

71. The Glass Is Half Full, Too

When negativists spill ice water on all your ideas

Other friends are demoralizing, robbing you of your confidence.

Several of your friends have a weekly get-together. You used to have fun kicking ideas around for little trips and short-term projects. But since Gail joined the group, she drains the energy right out of it. Every time you come up with a suggestion, she causes every scrap of enthusiasm to evaporate. She really believes none of you can control what she considers inevitable. And her pessimism is so convincing, you've given up on a lot of really promising ideas.

It'd be a little easier to take if Gail would make some effort to deal with a trouble spot. She's against everything that she herself doesn't handle. When she zaps every proposal by giving it quick burial, she offers nothing in its place.

You admit that sometimes her criticism is on the mark. If you could move from there, it'd be good. But Gail makes the comments personal and agitating. And you're all worn out from her barrage of "what ifs" and "it won't work."

THE GOAL

Salvage any useful negative points for a positive approach.

THE PLAN

1. *Lay the groundwork.* Rather than pushing for a particular proposal, which you know will be immediately shot down, build toward your plan. Realistically consider the specifics actually needed.

2. *Refuse to allow the wet blanket to interrupt you.* Keep talking, asking for fairness.

3. *Leave room for the negativist to back off.* Instead of saying she's wrong, acknowledge that trouble spots exist. Admit she may be right; however, you ask, what are the specific objections?

4. *Counteract pessimism with examples of what did work.* Resist inhaling the depressive air Gail creates by recalling similar precedents that were successful. At least reaffirm your belief that there are other possibilities to try.

Solomon Says:

When dealing with negativists:

- Aim to be realistic. Explore all aspects before announcing any solutions.

- It is this realism that provides balance between cockeyed optimists going off half-cocked and wet-blanket pessimists trying to drown any proposal they didn't initiate.

THE SCRIPT

YOU. Let's figure out what we'd need and how much time it would take to—

GAIL. It just won't work.

YOU. Let me finish, then you can talk.

GAIL. What's the use? There's no way around this.

YOU. Hold on a minute. What is it, specifically, that you're objecting to?

GAIL. We don't have enough experience or time for it to work.

YOU. [*friendly manner*]. That's a good point, Gail. We certainly would have to weigh that carefully. But let's take the worst-case scenario. What do we lose if we give it a try?

• • •

YOU. [*in private*]. Gail, we've been friends for quite a while, so I'd like to explain the frustration I've been feeling. I can't enjoy discussions when you limit your comments to doom and gloom. I know you bring out important points to consider, but do you think we can talk about a problem with an aim to solving it? Are you willing to give it a try?

GUIDELINE

Heed negativists only when they give specific objections.

These you can accept or reject. If they continue to tell you it can't work, point up the minimum danger and the value in trying.

72. Your Condescending Jokes Are Wearing Thin

When your friends know exactly which buttons to push

Why do some so-called friends keep pricking you with irritating humor?

Cass knows just the spots that will get a rise out of you. You can only guess why he gets pleasure subjecting you to this torment. You suspect he may be compensating for his own failures or trying to impress you with his superiority.

You didn't want to complain because the issues themselves aren't really a big deal. He chides you for being a sucker. Or hogging the conversation. Stuff like that. It's the constant daily attacks, however, that finally got to you. You blew up at what he claims is teasing but you felt was meant to hurt you.

You're aware that when he eggs you on, he's gleefully anticipating your reaction. If you question his intent, he says it was a joke. If that was a joke, why do you feel like punching him?

THE GOAL

Reduce the teasing.

THE PLAN

1. *Play a different tune.* Resist his ploy to unnerve you by not biting the bait. Don't attempt to defend yourself. Instead, shift the talk away from you to an impersonal discussion of the issue.

2. *Try friendly confrontation.* When you suspect he's using his pointed wit to have fun at your expense, concentrate on responding in a calm and pleasant tone. Keep asking him, repeatedly, to be more specific and elaborate on why he's formed that opinion.

3. *Give as well as you get.* Be ready next time to joke back and you'll take away his amusement. Laugh and it will sound like you're in on the joke. (Could it be that you *are* taking things too seriously and have to ease up?) If you can't think up a retort, then try a silent smile. Your body language should convey "I'm on to you, you're not getting to me any more."

THE SCRIPT

CASS. It's a good thing you're not in charge of buying the equipment. They really see you coming.

YOU. [*ignoring the charge*]. What do you think should be the main considerations for the purchase?

CASS. [*persisting*]. First, not to be buffaloed. Every salesperson who sees you must say, 'I've got a live one.'

YOU. Level with me, Cass. You may think that's a joke, but did you mean to insult me? Why are you using your jokes to keep putting me down?

CASS. How'd you get a crazy idea like that!?

YOU. [*laughing*]. You sound like I believe the moon is made of green cheese. If there's a problem here, I wish you'd come right out with it. Specifically, what are your objections to my handling this matter?

CASS. No problem. I guess it was a bad joke after all.

GUIDELINE

You are who you are—don't try to fit others' perceptions of you.

Hecklers and needlers only tease those who react defensively. So lighten up.

73. That's Not Amusing

*Blunting the point of your
friend's critical wit*

At times, the jokes go beyond a friend's toying with you. They are cover-ups for flat-out criticism.

Pat is being destructively clever. He knows you hate looking foolish or embarrassed—that you'll suffer his veiled taunts because you can't prove they're anything but clever jabs. You're afraid if you don't go along, you'll be called a poor sport.

You'd like to expose the sham jokes for what they are—glaring criticism. He's hiding his fault-finding behind a smile. And you're wondering why he's using sarcastic wit to attack you. Does he harbor deep feelings about you that he can't bring himself to deal with on a conscious level?

How can you outsmart his pointed comments without getting stabbed yourself?

THE GOAL
Handle the criticism effectively.

THE PLAN
1. *Sift and shift.* Concentrate on the meaning behind the joke instead of your hurt feelings. Listen to hear if there's some grain of truth in all that mumbo jumbo. Instead of worrying about how you'll respond, pay attention to the words.

2. *Think positively.* In personal relationships, two negatives don't make a positive. Accusing and blaming someone who upsets you won't help, but changing your reaction can.

3. *Politely and directly say what's on your mind.* Releasing the anger and frustration that's been building up can reverse an unpleasant situation. You can stand up for yourself and still respect the rights of your friend.

4. *Practice several retorts when you're alone.* You know the general areas he's going to torture you with. Figure out right now how you are going to respond next time.

THE SCRIPT

PAT. That's some outfit you put together. Where was the fire sale?

YOU. [*Maybe your choice is a little far out, but certainly not tacky, as Pat implies.*] Down on Fifth and Main. I'll call you next time so I can help you pick out something just as funky.

• • •

PAT. You really know how to welcome new members [*you having remained silent when some came over*]. I'm going to nominate you for Mr. Congeniality.

YOU. I accept your nomination. But tell me, where did you study diplomacy? And you know, Pat, you were talking so much, I couldn't find an opening to jump in.

• • •

PAT. What's the matter with you lately?

YOU. Since you asked, I'll tell you. I don't find your ridicule very funny. I think you'd find me more cooperative if you toned it down a little.

GUIDELINE
Return the sting by poking fun yourself.
This won't change your friend, but at least you'll stop smarting from the jabs.

74. Please Listen to Me

When your friend becomes unsupportive and inattentive

Some friendships grow in different directions and no longer meet each other's needs.

You and Sara and Helen have been friends since college. You used to call yourselves the Three Musketeers. Last month Helen moved away. With one-third of the equation missing, you and Sara don't seem to click any more.

There's no real communication, just frustration and regret. You used to have such good times. Always something to laugh about. Always some late news to share.

Now when you talk to Sara, it's as though she's somewhere else. Either she's not listening or she's condescending and preachy. She makes you feel you're being childish to feel hurt or angry when you tell her about a problem. You find yourself editing your remarks before you speak. The free give-and-take conversations are gone.

You'd like to resolve this difficulty, but so far both of you are pretending nothing has changed. You don't know how to broach the subject.

THE GOAL
Reconnect a waning friendship.

THE PLAN
1. *Examine what you give to each other.* The basis of a friendship is mutual satisfaction. What is it that you are able to give your friend? Is it support, being a good audience, good ideas? What do you get from her? Is it advice, book and movie critiques, companionship? Figure out when you feel better for having been with her.

2. *Identify what you find annoying.* She's never on time and keeps you waiting? She can be rude to strangers? Sometimes she acts

holier-than-thou? The benefits should outweigh the irritations if you're going to make the effort to administer CPR to this friendship.

3. *Tell your friend how you feel.* Ask her if she's experiencing similar feelings. It's possible you just need more time to adjust to being a pair instead of a group of three.

4. *Talk about whatever you used to enjoy doing.* Discuss the sharing of ideas and decisions. Whatever it was—the laughs you had mimicking stuffed shirts, the exchange of gossip, the answers to political problems. Then decide together where you want to go from here.

THE SCRIPT

YOU. Sara, I think it's time we level with each other. Ever since Helen left, you and I don't seem to get along as well as we used to. Is it my imagination or are you sensing the same thing?

SARA. I didn't realize before how much of a cohesive force Helen was. I guess she was the one who made us laugh at ourselves.

YOU. I know we'll always remain friends, but do we want to work at being close friends? I know there are things we enjoy about each other and things that upset us.

SARA. Well, why don't we put all our cards on the table. What do I do that you like and what bugs you?

YOU. OK, I'd like to feel when I tell you about my achievements that you know I'm not bragging and you're genuinely happy for me. Also, when I talk about my problems, it seems to me you make light of them, and that's demeaning.

SARA. I had no idea I did that. Now it's my turn. . .

[*The back and forth continues until they decide it is worth the trouble to try to regain lost ground.*]

GUIDELINE

In an ongoing relationship, weigh your present needs.

An open and frank discussion will help you decide what kind of future relationship you care to pursue.

Chapter XIV

Neighbors

The problem with neighbors is that you're stuck with them for an undetermined period of time. You have enough stress in your life without having to come home to any more. So if you have no intention of moving in the near future, you certainly need to resolve some of the difficulties.

Blaring, uncontrolled noise rates as one of the top sources of misery. Usually, this is an inconsiderate act rather than an intentional attempt to split open your eardrums.

Some neighbors are slobs and there goes the neighborhood. Others are terribly neat and if you happen to leave something on their turf, watch out! A nasty dispute may escalate. And then there are the friendly souls who keep borrowing and never return. Really, you can't keep replacing these items.

Today, with so many people working all or part-time from their homes, interruptions from next door have become a problem. You don't want to be rude, but you have to get your work done.

These are the kinds of troublesome situations discussed in Chapter XIV.

75. Can You Keep It Down to a Dull Roar?

Dealing with the vein-popping noise from next door

Maybe your neighbors, the Stacks, never heard of the Golden Rule. If they have, they've certainly tarnished their end of it.

You refrained from complaining about the blaring music at the pool party that lasted till midnight. You knew it was just an occasional offense, although you wish they had forewarned you. You'd have planned an escape for the evening.

You love well-modulated music, listening to the selections *you* have chosen. But when piercing sounds from someone else's radio or stereo penetrate your closed windows as you're trying to watch TV, you want to scream at the inconsiderate boobs.

Now, however, you know you have to do something because the Stacks are interfering with your sleep. Sunday morning is the only time you can get some extra shuteye. Why must they use those couple of hours to mow the lawn? And don't they realize when their dog is outside late at night baying at the moon it is keeping their neighbors awake and plotting revenge? You're reluctant to confront the Stacks since you have to continue living next door to them. Is there anything else you can do?

THE GOAL
Reduce the clamor amicably.

THE PLAN
1. *Decide if the noise is deliberate or insensitive.* In most cases, people like the Stacks are oblivious to the harm resulting from their toxic behavior. They live in their own little world and need to be reminded of the reality. This can come in the form of a polite request. Face-to-face is better than a phone call, at least initially, because you'll be able to see as well as hear the reaction.

2. *Consider other action if your request is ignored.* If you live in an apartment, notify the manager. Noisy neighbors may violate terms of the lease. If you are part of a homeowners association, check for antinoise rules and regulations. When these infuriators are told to cool it by a third party, it takes the onus off your back.

3. *Call the police as a last resort.* If the disturbance continues at unreasonable hours, this probably breaks a local ordinance. When the voice of authority shows up on the doorstep, the offender doesn't know which neighbor sounded the alarm.

THE SCRIPT

YOU. Mr. Stack, I'm sure you don't realize this, but the loud noises coming from your home are upsetting your neighbors.

STACK. What are you talking about?

YOU. Well, for one thing, your dog's barking late at night wakes up my baby and then we all have a problem getting back to sleep. Also, Sunday is the only day I can sleep a little later, but the lawnmower makes that impossible. Could we work out something reasonable? Perhaps take your dog inside after nine and wait until nine to start cutting the grass?

STACK. I can take the dog in earlier, but if I wait until nine to mow, it gets too hot.

YOU. Maybe you could do this after dinner when the sun goes down? We really need our sleep!

• • •

YOU. [*telephone call to Mr. Stack at 11.00 P.M.*]. Mr. Stack, your dog is barking and it's keeping us up. Could you please quiet him? [*or*] The music is very loud. Could you please turn down the sound? [*If necessary, repeat the call or notify police.*]

GUIDELINE
Use the polite request to avoid a future feud.
Only if that doesn't work, take additional steps to stop the noise.

76. I Know You Must Have Forgotten, But...

Keeping the perennial borrower from taking advantage.

You, by nature, are friendly and helpful. So you hate to say no.

Chuck is a great guy, but he's a moocher, a sponger, a parasite. He doesn't buy, he borrows. Then he forgets to return your hammer, your drill, your clippers. Whenever you're missing a tool or equipment, you remember where it is—at Chuck's.

You know he's taking advantage of your good nature. But you haven't figured out if he's just habitually inconsiderate—blissfully unaware of his exploitative behavior—or being deliberately manipulative.

You want to put a stop to this borrowing, but you can't figure out a way to do it that would avoid an argument.

THE GOAL

Remain friends while stopping your neighbor from taking advantage.

THE PLAN

1. *Pretend the imposition is unintentional.* Don't let your annoyance reach the boiling point or one day you'll explode. No need to counter-attack. Try other ways to be assertive and get your point across, such as good-natured teasing.

2. *Politely refuse the next request.* And the next, and the one after that. Up until now, you've never opened your mouth to protest. Maybe he's been thinking you're a generous guy who likes to share. While you never need a reason to turn down a request, you can soften your refusal by putting it between two suggestions.

3. *Turn the tables with a request of your own.* For example, ask about jointly purchasing some equipment. Discuss a barter arrangement.

THE SCRIPT

CHUCK. The blade on my saw is dull. Could I use yours to finish cutting extra shelves for my closet?

YOU. [*smiling*]. Chuck, if you borrow one more thing from me, I'm going to charge you a rental fee. What do you think the going rate is?

• • •

YOU. I can see you need the saw, but I'm going to be using it today. How about asking Jason across the street?

• • •

YOU. Chuck, I've had so many requests from neighbors to borrow my tools that I've had to start a new policy. Sometimes the stuff comes back dulled or damaged, so I decided I can't lend them out any more. I'm sorry.

• • •

YOU. Chuck, I'm going to need a new leaf blower. Since you don't have one, what do you say we split the cost and buy one for the two of us?

GUIDELINE

People won't walk all over you if you show them they're out of step. Speak up.

77. I Value Our Friendship, But I've Got to Work, Too

Protecting your time while operating a home-based business

Taking away your things is not nearly as upsetting to you as taking away your time.

Some people refuse to hear the message until you hit them with a sledgehammer. They just can't take a hint. Before you started working at home, you and Donna used to get together on weekends to catch up on the neighborhood news or attend events. Now you need every minute to concentrate on business.

But Donna still finds a dozen excuses to keep popping in during the week. You've explained to her why you can't talk. She invariably keeps chatting until you practically throw her out and she leaves angry.

You enjoy Donna's company and going to neighborhood activities with her, but you don't know how you can fit her into your weekends or control her weekday interruptions.

THE GOAL

Work undisturbed by interruptions.

THE PLAN

1. *Designate specific times to talk.* Obviously Donna still enjoys talking to you and misses the former get-togethers. You're treating her like an addict who has to quit cold turkey. Figure out a minimum time block when it's convenient for you to take a needed break and socialize.

2. *Agree to some variation of the office open door* (open, I'm available; closed, don't even think about it). You might hang colored cards on your front door knob (green, ring; red, go away) as a pre-arranged signal. Treat home office intruders as you would office interrupters. In the office you make it clear to the kibitzer (she has a better way to handle your job; he needs a warm-up chat before he can get to work) to leave you alone because you're really swamped. Or you go hide in the conference room. At home, you simply hide from the rest of the world.

3. *Take control of your environment.* Lock your door and pretend you're not home. Assuming you have a separate business phone, turn on your home telephone answering machine so that you can screen your calls and be alert to any emergencies.

Solomon Says:

Try a two-pronged approach with interrupters:

1. Gently stop the interruption. Don't open your door; talk through the window and then you can walk away.

2. Arrange a change that will minimize future interruptions. Offer those specific times that you'll be free and where you want to meet elsewhere.

THE SCRIPT

DONNA. I don't understand why you're being so mean. Are you angry? Have I offended you?

YOU. Oh, Donna, please understand how little time I have now that I work at home. It has nothing to do with you or my enjoying your company as always.

DONNA. But you never have any time for me at all. I really miss our talks.

YOU. I do, too. Tell you what. If it's okay with you, let's set aside a half-hour on Saturday mornings for a coffee break. I'll stop by your house at ten o'clock and we'll be able to keep in touch. [*It's much easier for you to get up and leave from her home then to get her out of yours.*]

GUIDELINE

It's up to you to control those interruptions.
Don't respond, or plan ahead to meet elsewhere.

78. Cut Me Some Slack, Jack

*When neighbors are unreasonable
and won't budge an inch*

Is it your misfortune to live next door to rigidity and vindictiveness personified?

Your next door neighbor, Rubin, is extremely protective of his turf. If anything of yours is one inch over the property line, forget it, you'll never see it again. When your fruit tree arches over to his property, expect to see the extension chopped off. Your kid's little red wagon disappeared and you suspect little Andy parked it in the neighbor's driveway.

When you accused Rubin of taking the wagon, he vowed to get even. The next day you assume it was his dog who was digging up your yard. This led to an argument and then he started spreading ugly stories about you and your wife. The party you had lasted after 11:00 P.M. and he called the police claiming a disturbance.

You made an attempt to reason with him. You told him he had to learn to bend a little to get along in this world. This made it worse because he was insulted. He claimed that you implied he was pig-headed.

Neither family intends to move. You are at an impasse. What can you do?

THE GOAL
Devise alternative means to resolve disputes.

THE PLAN
1. *First, you have to win his trust.* He won't listen to any suggestion you have until he believes you're sincere and not trying to take advantage of him by blurring the boundary line. In a light tone, ask him why he always seems mad at you. Then let him release the anger he

appears to feel. If you have done something wrong, apologize and move on.

2. *Let him salvage his pride.* Stop telling him he's wrong. Instead offer a gracious way out. Disarm him by gently massaging his ego with an honest compliment—there must be *something* about him that you admire. Show him you respect his opinion even though you don't agree. Give him the opportunity to be a part of solving the difficulties.

3. *Recognize his concerns.* Appeal to what he wants in a polite, positive, and relaxed manner. Show him how to get this and then how both of you would benefit. Suggest an alternative way of handling your disagreements. Wedge in the negative consequences if you can't agree.

Solomon Says:

Use the trial-run technique on stubborn people:

- Let them feel they're still in control. After hearing their expressions of anger or resentment, don't tell them what to do.

- Instead, suggest an alternative procedure with a limited time for the test. The trial run plan is then easily rejected if it doesn't prove mutually beneficial.

THE SCRIPT

YOU.   Rubin, we've been going at each other for a couple of months. How about telling me what I'm doing that's making you seem so angry.

RUBIN.   That's easy. Where do I start? Why can't you stay on your side? You're always intruding onto my property. I guess what makes me so mad is that you're always imposing instead of following the rules.

YOU.   OK, I guess I haven't been overly careful. If that offends you, I'm sorry and I'll try harder. I'm sure you're a reasonable person, so let's talk about this, Rubin. Obviously, we have different approaches, but I respect your opinion even when we don't agree. What would you like to have happen? Where should we go from here?

RUBIN. Well, tell me what I'm supposed to do when your stuff ends up on my side?

YOU. How about getting two little red flags, one for each of us. When something upsetting happens, either of us can put up the flag, then we'll talk it out later. But when we come home from work, neither of us wants any more tension. Am I right?

RUBIN. It would be nice to come home to a friendly street.

GUIDELINE
Point out a direction without pointing out who's to blame.

79. Oh Boy, Just What I Wanted

*When they bring their dogs
to perform in your yard*

Whatever the regulation is in your locality, this is something you don't want to suffer.

Although your neighbor Glen has a large backyard, he uses your front lawn for Scottie. It has become the terrier's personal toilet.

This has been going on every day until the grass is so decorated with these droppings that it's unusable and, what's worse, an unsightly, smelly health hazard.

Glen's behavior is obnoxious, but you don't know how to approach your neighbor. You're afraid if you antagonize him, the poop might start appearing right outside your front door.

Is there some way to get through to him?

THE GOAL

Keep your yard from being converted to a pet's open-air outhouse.

THE PLAN

1. *Do the research.* If you have a neighborhood association, it may have pooper-scooper rules. Your city or county probably has an ordinance making the behavior unlawful and punishable by fine. Videotape the offense. If the meeting doesn't produce the desired change, notify the government department that has animal control jurisdiction to enforce the law and fine the offender.

2. *Rally the troops.* If your adjacent neighbors are also being abused, invite them to a meeting at your home to discuss "a neighborhood problem." Include Glen to give him a chance to be part of the solution.

3. *Stand up and speak out.* If you alone are being victimized, calmly but assertively, confront the culprit. Force him to try to defend himself and admit his misconduct. Suggest a more appropriate way to act.

Solomon Says:

Remember this:

- If you have a problem affecting other neighbors, you reduce the risk of retaliation by exerting group pressure.

- If the problem is yours alone, then you have to confront— calmly and firmly.

THE SCRIPT

YOU. [*at the meeting with your neighbors*]. The problem we're here to discuss is how to resolve a health hazard. As you've all noticed, some of our lawns are unusable because they have become public potties for pets. [*Continue without ever looking at Glen.*] Neighbors who leave our lawns and sidewalks in a mess may not realize the seriousness of their actions. It is so serious, that our local ordinance states: [*quote the law*] and this is punishable by a $x fine. [*Glen will get the message.*]

What steps do you think we can take to establish our own pooper-scooper rules without resorting to reporting the offense to the authorities? [*Remain courteous and calm and in control of the meeting.*]

YOU. [*talking privately to Glen*]. Could it possibly be some oversight that you've confused my front lawn as an extension of your own?

GLEN. What in the world are you talking about?

YOU. My lawn has become a cesspool because of your dog's droppings! Why are you using my yard for your dog? This is totally unacceptable and, besides, there's a local ordinance prohibiting such action.

GLEN. I hadn't realized. . .

YOU: [*remembering your goal*]. Okay, but now that you do, let's get one thing straight. Where will you be walking—and cleaning up after—your dog from now on?

GUIDELINE

Offer the offender a chance to change before calling the authorities.

Part C

Additional Techniques to Deal with Infuriating Situations

Since you really can't change difficult people, this potpourri of ideas is offered to help you control your response to them. In doing so, you will improve the results or consequences.

This closing part of the book looks at times you feel

- intimidated and afraid to talk to your boss,

- enraged, but you don't want to blow your cool,

- anxious to remember some information to ease the tension,

- compelled to improve worker morale,

- lacking strategies for talking to teens.

The final section, "In Conclusion, A Dozen Important Reminders," reviews ways to move from circular thinking (you're not getting anywhere—just going around in circles) to strategic, targeted talking (what to do and say to get what you hope to accomplish).

80. Overcoming the Fear of Approaching Your Boss

The key words to remember are *preparation* and *practice*. The following steps will help you feel confident rather than intimidated by your boss.

1. CAMPAIGN FOR APPROVAL FROM DAY ONE ON THE JOB.

- Believe that you deserve respect. You won't be treated with respect unless you expect it. If you stand up for yourself while honoring another's right to oppose you, your intimidator will admire your strength. And don't be surprised if such a boss becomes your mentor.

- Take the initiative to separate yourself from the pack. Keep your comments at meetings constructive, sharp, and to the point. Think through what you'll say before you talk so that you keep within one minute. If you develop this habit, when you speak, others will listen.

- Submit unsolicited proposals and recommendations. Do this throughout the year for the boss's consideration. Don't wait for an invitation in order to demonstrate that you want to help your organization. Getting your well-thought-out idea accepted isn't as important as showing you're a creative thinker. Work on increasing your visibility.

- Suggest and volunteer. Offer to chair ad hoc committees that make recommendations to the boss. Share credit with your colleagues in the reports. How you helped solve company problems will become important during performance evaluations and raise requests.

- Stand up to your boss. When you disagree, tactfully and politely point out how the idea being discussed won't help the boss achieve expressed goals.

2. STUDY TRENDS.

- Learn the direction being taken by your company and in your field. Read publications as well as quarterly and annual reports.

- Determine what new skills you'll need to keep up. Specifically, what are the requirements for the next level that you'll have to learn.

- Take advantage of training. Check out what's available through your company. If your company doesn't provide this, consider getting training on your own, but find out if, at least, you'll be allowed time off to attend. Stress the benefit to the organization.

3. REDESIGN YOUR JOB CLOSER TO YOUR CAREER GOALS.

- Eliminate your insignificant tasks. Make time to concentrate on major ones that you can combine with needed new tasks.

- Search for ways to fill your company's needs. Volunteer, without being asked, to take over work that's piling up due to an unfilled slot.

- Invent a job that directly meets a company problem. Question your boss to learn his/her needs in meeting personal goals.

4. TRAIN OTHERS FOR YOUR JOB.

- Free yourself to move up. Teach a subordinate how to do your job. You won't move up if the boss thinks you can't be replaced.

- Watch for a line position opening. You'll climb higher and be paid more than if you are staff support.

5. INCREASE YOUR CONTACTS.

- Network both within and outside the company.

- Keep making friends and doing favors. Collect the chits, but don't remind people that they owe you.

6. COMPILE SALARY STATISTICS.

- Do the research. Prepare a pay chart showing current rates in your field and geographic area. Learn what the local competition is paying.
- Secure information from your personal network.
- Check the Internet for job search data.
- Get figures on annual pay surveys. Review major business and professional publications. Insert talk about articles you've read into conversations with your boss.

7. PREPARE EVIDENCE FOR A RAISE REQUEST.

- Besides the pay chart, your package should highlight how your special capabilities led to specified accomplishments. Quantify when possible.
- Relate these achievements to company goals.
- Include commendations from customers and colleagues.

8. PREPARE YOUR SALES PITCH.

- Stress the mutual benefit in helping your boss be more successful.
- Ask what other skills you should acquire.
- Express eagerness for challenging new assignments.
- Offer a what-have-you-got-to-lose trial run. You'll do your work plus extra for a stated time. If satisfactory, you get the agreed reward; if not, there's no risk to the boss.
- Remember, your raise hinges on one thing—your value to the organization. What you need or want or your past dedication is not a deciding factor.

9. PRACTICE, PRACTICE, PRACTICE.

- Rehearse at home. Use bullet notes. It's okay to refer to them during your actual meetings.
- Tape-record yourself. Speak up, slow down, but keep your enthusiasm.

- Role-play with a friend. Take turns being the boss. Maintain eye contact with your partner. Practice body language that shows you're sure of yourself. Stand and sit up straight. Think up a little banter you can use—that also shows you feel confident.

10. MAKE AN APPOINTMENT.

- Determine the day and time when the boss is least busy.
- Ask for a few uninterrupted minutes of the boss's time.
- Go—you're ready and set. Good luck.

81. Managing Your Own Anger

1. FREEZE. STAND MUTE WHEN CRITICISM IS PIERCING.

Your pulse is racing and you're ready to lash out at the one causing you pain. Take a few deep breaths. To keep your temper in check, chant a few words such as, "Take control, take control, take control."

Admit to yourself you're angry. If you simmer until you finally explode, you may take out your anger on an innocent person. So figure out what's really bothering you. Take a short walk or talk this over with someone you trust or write a letter to vent your anger and then tear it up.

Be clear about your goal. Telling someone off gives momentary satisfaction and brings a bigger headache. What do you really want? A stupid mistake corrected? An account saved after an important order was delayed? To influence a poor attitude?

Be ready to discuss what you believe should be done or how this situation should be handled in the future.

2. ASK YOUR CRITIC TO BE MORE SPECIFIC.

Extract as much information as you can. You want to be perfectly clear about the action being criticized. There may be something about the situation you want to change. Perhaps you misinterpreted what was said. A remark you found infuriating may not have been meant as a personal criticism, but was caused by a system or condition needing alteration.

This incident can serve to identify the problem and resolve built-up resentment. Once you calm down, you'll want to consider if there is any validity to the criticism. Everyone's reality is different, based on experiences unique to each individual.

3. LIMIT COMMENTS TO THE CURRENT ISSUE.

Don't dredge up garbage and irrelevant past mistakes. If you can't let go of a grudge, you're allowing your nemesis to have control over you. If your critic gets defensive, rephrase your remark and set a time to discuss unresolved grievances.

4. USE QUESTIONS TO AVOID DIRECT ACCUSATIONS.

Talk it out. Hear the other side. Listen for the emotion being expressed. You don't have to agree to acknowledge another's feelings. ("I can see you're upset and you feel I was insensitive.") Try to understand why the incident happened.

5. DIG OUT THE FACTS WHILE PRESERVING PRIDE.

("You know, of course, how vital it was for this order to be filled today. Please tell me, why didn't it go out?") Couple your criticism with an offer of help. Show some sensitivity. Be civil, with no threatening tone or personal attack ("How stupid can you be?"). Discuss the behavior without name-calling. Such phrases as "That might be so in many instances, but in this case. . ." or "Maybe so, but it seems to me that. . ." will soften your remarks and let the other save face.

6. ARTICULATE YOUR FEELINGS.

Calmly state how the infuriator's behavior made you feel ("I felt hurt when. . .") rather than counterattack ("Only a selfish lug would have forgotten our anniversary"). You can't assume to know what someone else is feeling. So don't tell what another is feeling or should feel.

7. REFRAIN FROM GIVING UNASKED-FOR ADVICE.

Often when people express their feelings, they're not looking for answers. They simply want to share how they feel. They don't want you to tell them, "You shouldn't feel upset," or, "This is what you should do." If you offer advice without being asked, they feel you're putting them down.

8. MAKE ASSUMPTIONS BASED ON PAST BEHAVIORS.

You can make an educated guess on the expected response. You've seen it before. If you do A, he'll probably do B. This is a valuable tool to use. Think this through. What would have to happen to change this person's feelings or alter this bad situation? Make notes on what works for you.

9. SUGGEST A POSITIVE SOLUTION OR A BETTER OPTION.

When you express your anger creatively, that's generating healthy energy. Once you pinpoint the problem, the tension spurs you on to find ways to solve it or to improve a miserable situation. You can now break down the barriers and get a really good dialogue with both of you contributing to the resolution. It sure beats being immobilized, feeling victimized, and plotting revenge. Taking responsibility for the rotten situation even though you didn't cause it will give you a feeling of control.

10. USE HUMOR TO EASE THE TENSION.

Laughter elevates everybody's mood. Presidential politics gives us many examples of how wit is used to defuse anger. John F. Kennedy reportedly remarked, "I used to wonder when I was a member of the House how President Truman got in so much trouble. Now I am beginning to get the idea. It is not difficult." When General McClellan, in command of the Union forces during the Civil War, was so overly cautious that he didn't do anything but wait, Abe Lincoln wrote him, "If you don't want to use the Army, I should like to borrow it for a while."

11. CONSERVE YOUR ENERGY.

Use it wisely to gather your information, to strategize the best approach and devise a plan of action. Stop kicking yourself if you made a mistake—we all make mistakes. You'll learn for the next time. Now go forward and do something to make things better.

82. Lowering Hostility by Retrieving the Right Words

A simple and quick mental retrieval system lets you instantly recall personal data you've stored. During a confrontation or conversation, this can increase your influence, reduce hostility, and win over adversaries.

By pushing a button in your brain so that the right words pop out of your emergency shelf, you're able to link what you say to your listener's interests.

Rather than depending on luck, you prepare for, recognize, and are quick enough to grab opportunities. It's a matter of targeting and depositing useful information about people for a later time.

STEPS

1. *Choose a filing system you find most comfortable.* You have to store information for future use. Some people still prefer a color-coded notebook or index file over a computerized version. Whatever you decide, this is where you deposit data about people you've targeted.

2. *Decide who should be in this central intelligence file.* Who can influence your future? You might start with your boss, advisors, and opinion molders. A gradually expanded file could include executives, colleagues, subordinates, company task forces members, neighbors, community volunteers, and members of your church, club, and business or professional association.

3. *Consider the types of information you'll collect.* Besides bits about business, professional, educational, or family, you may find it useful to know the people they associate with, special projects they're interested in, proud accomplishments, chief concerns, prime priorities, and the pressures they face and from whom.

4. *Determine sources of information.* Gather your research by scouring company reports and newsletters, television and radio shows, business and professional journals, relevant items from the Internet, business and gossip columns in newspapers, notes on activities and opinions in magazines. After exchanging business cards during a

conversation, jot down on the back of your contact's card (or on one of yours if they have none) any names that were mentioned of their spouses, kids, associates, interests, or organizations.

5. *Utilize clippings.* After entering your information, forward the clipping to the person named along with an appropriate note. This is a good ice-breaker.

6. *Enter "I shoulda saids."* When you finish licking your wounds after a lost battle, review and appreciate the agonizing experience as a valuable lesson. Record what you'll say when a similar situation arises again.

EXAMPLES

Now you need ways to jog your memory. The key is instant linkage: Associate the new information with something you already know. Try forming a mental picture, the crazier the better.

- You and Mike, a neighbor, had a tiff a while back over a proposed zoning change and haven't spoken since. You read about his son Fredric getting hurt in a football game. Picture Mike taking a ridiculous ten-foot ballet leap to catch a pass from Fredric. That image will surface when you see Mike again. You'll remember to ask about Fredric and recalling Fredric's name will be impressive.

- From a local televised panel show you learned that Donna, your adversary, is an avid environmentalist. You want to remember to discuss with her some relevant ideas to show you have interests in common that might stop the bickering. You imagine one idea linked to the next—some kind of goofy story—and you'll be amazed how much you'll recall without any notes before you. (You see Donna at the office buried under tons of wasted paper that you are suctioning off, etc.)

- Jay has been stand-offish and you sense he doesn't like you, although you have never had a one-on-one conversation with him. You clipped an article from *Business Week* and sent it to him. The next time you meet, you remember to congratulate him on becoming the new coordinator of the centralized message project and the impact that will have. Everyone hungers for recognition; he'll eat it up.

83. Reducing Worker Frustration with Effective Policies

Many organizations have implemented some of the following methods that proved successful in improving boss/employee relationships. These ideas have reinvigorated demotivated workers and reduced tension in the workplace.

1. PROVIDING STRESS REDUCERS

- better insurance coverage
- improved retirement plans
- a child-care center on premises or nearby
- a well-equipped exercise room
- organizing team sports

2. ALLOWING MORE FLEXIBLE SCHEDULES

- a policy permitting time-off when necessary
- authorizing four ten-hour workdays with Fridays off or the option of working one day a week at home
- casual dress code when not expecting clients

3. CLEARLY DEFINING CAREER TRACKS

- telling when and why raises and promotions are given
- paying part or all of tuition to encourage continuous learning and to develop additional skills
- establishing an office library with helpful books, magazines, and audio and visual material
- having a ceremony to award certificates for completing a training program
- assigning an experienced worker to coach a new employee

4. REWARDING PRODUCTIVITY

- a clear, simple, realistic incentive plan with updated score-card to keep employees informed of progress
- planning monthly meetings that mix fun and business—gift certificates, balloons, singing, hoopla when giving awards for problem solving
- arranging monthly lunches for the staff to announce meeting production and sales goals
- providing an expense account
- giving an extra vacation day for each quarter that the company shows increased profit
- split the savings when employees can help reduce costs
- use of a company car
- assigning a better office
- closing the shop for the day and taking the staff to a movie, concert, or professional sports event

5. MAKING EMPLOYEE ACHIEVEMENTS VISIBLE

- challenging high achievers by giving them the chance to help solve difficult problems
- asking coworkers to nominate the individual or team who presented the best innovation to improve service, cut costs, or suggested a new product
- inviting a worker to present his/her good idea to the board
- changing the job title and work location; putting the employee's name on letterhead, door, or business cards
- having the head honcho publicly acknowledge workers who've done a really fine job
- the president sending a warm note or making a personal phone call to express appreciation
- publicizing names and pictures of outstanding workers through the local media and in the organization's newsletter
- rewarding the employee who performs an act of kindness with a monthly gift certificate
- providing a designated parking space

84. More Tips for Talking to Teens

1. *Give your teens your continual, frequent feedback.* They need to hear the good as well as the bad—just the way you need feedback at work. How you talk to your teens at this stage will affect your relationship when they're older. Let them know it's okay to have a different opinion and you're glad to discuss it.

2. **Forget about getting blind obedience.** Your aim is to really hear what each other is saying. Listen to yourself giving orders. Is that the manner you use with your friends when you criticize and praise?

3. *Be straightforward.* Stop playing games: hedging when they make requests, giving hope when you know you'll refuse, offering a choice when there isn't one. Don't say, "When you get a chance, I'd like you to. . ." when you need it done now.

4. *Reduce your rules to a short written list.* Post it, saying, "This is a copy of what we agreed on. Please look it over to see that it's accurate, and then sign it."

5. *Be consistent, firm, and friendly.* Don't make threats and then give in. What's right today isn't wrong tomorrow. Deliver your no's in a kind and understanding voice. Keep your demands to a minimum and make your teens aware that they are not solely on their own, not completely free to do as they want.

6. *Keep your statements unambiguous.* Be direct, but friendly. Spell out what you expect—who, what, when, how much. Clear, simple, and straightforward. Muddied messages lead to hurt or belligerent feelings.

7. *Be clear on the consequences.* If the rules are broken, you both know what will happen. Then enforce your rules. Don't sell compliance with bribes, promises, or a long list of reasons, and don't get into a debate about it. However, if your teen comes up with good justification, be willing to be flexible and modify your rule.

8. *Take responsibility for your decision.* Don't make your teen shunt back and forth, asking you and then the other parent. If you have to talk things over with your spouse, say so.

9. *Offer praise without comparisons.* Don't couple it with criticism,

for example, saying that something was good, not like her past mistakes. Don't pour forth criticism you've been saving up.

10. *Resist hurtful name-calling.* Especially watch out when you're too exhausted to deal with a request you made that is not being obeyed. Don't be a doomsday parent. Teens are very sensitive to criticism.

11. *Understand teenagers are struggling to be independent.* In the search for their identity, they move between acting like children and grown-ups, or they try to be both simultaneously. They don't want to share every detail and hate feeling they're being cross-examined. To them, it means you don't trust their judgment. Respect their need for privacy—their room is their sanctuary.

12. *Realize they long to be accepted without question.* Balance their great desire to fit in by helping them develop self-confidence, not being dependent on external things for self-esteem.

13. *Help them learn ways to express their emotions.* Through good discussions, show them how to resolve conflicts constructively.

14. *Let them know you take seriously what they say.* Really listen to them. Be nonjudgmental in your response. That is important to them; they want to be heard. They want to know you honestly care about their ideas.

15. *Give your child the same respect and understanding you'd give a friend.* Reject an inappropriate action without making the teen feel rejected.

16. *Resist teen manipulation.* React calmly and don't bite when you hear any of the following:

- *threats* to quit school or leave home. Be matter of fact and return the focus to problem-solving.

- *guilt* as in, "If you really cared about me, you'd. . ." Try, "I do care about you, that's why I'm. . ."

- *comparison* as in, "Everyone else has a ticket to. . ." Cut this short with, "I've spoken to some of the other parents and we agreed that's not suitable for your age."

- *lying.* When they deny the obvious, counter with, "Here, look at the facts that dispute that. Now the question is what should we do next?" Let your teen suggest a fair and reasonable punishment or take part in establishing the rules he's to live by. Explain that rules must be obeyed, just like when you're playing baseball.

TO IMPROVE YOUR WAY OF COMMUNICATING

Instead of saying: Try saying:

- How about starting your homework?
- It's 7 P.M. Time to start your homework.

- This time I mean it. Turn off the TV or you'll be sorry.
- Okay, you decide. Turn off the TV now or you won't be allowed to watch TV the whole weekend.

- Clean up your room and I'll get you tickets to the concert.
- Clean up your room as you promised. Then we'll discuss the concert.

- Cindy has such good manners. Why can't you be more like her?
- Cindy is so pleasant. I really enjoy talking to her.

- Everyone of us in the Matson family has been an honor student. We expect the same from you. Just study harder.
- I know math is tough for you. Would you like Tommy to come over and study with you?

- What's that drawing supposed to be? Is it lopsided or do I have it upside down?
- This drawing is different. Tell me about it. (Show interest and encourage; don't ridicule.)

- I don't want to hear any more about it. You know the rule.
- Okay, I'm listening to your objection. State your case and then I'll decide.

- Now that's the way it should look. Why can't you do it like that all the time?
- I noticed you did that really well. Looks great. I'm so proud of the way you handled it.

- There you go, messing up again. You're making me crazy! I don't know what to do with you!
- If there's anything I can do to make you feel more comfortable, let me know. I love you and I'm glad to help.

85. In Conclusion: A Dozen Important Reminders

1. YOU CAN CHANGE ONLY WHAT YOU CAN CONTROL— YOUR THOUGHTS, WORDS, AND ACTIONS.

You can't change other people, but you can influence them by altering their perceptions of you. If they expect you to argue, counter-charge, or act intimidated and you react differently, they'll be thrown off balance and see you in a new light. When possible, use humor to reduce the stress. Ease a tense situation by laughing at yourself. One way is to recall an embarrassing incident.

2. CHANGE TO A RESPONSE THAT GETS ATTENTION.

Be civil, gracious, positive, straightforward—in words and body language. Call people by their correct names. Pay attention, trying to understand rather than waiting to pounce with a counterdefense. Show how they can get what they want by helping you get what you want. Blame an intangible (e.g., a poor system) to avoid blaming a person. Finger-pointing just escalates tension. Stick to the facts. Help others feel good about themselves by expressing honest appreciation—there must be one quality you can be sincere about!

3. FREEZE—WHAT YOU DON'T SAY CAN'T BE USED AGAINST YOU.

Only in extreme emergencies do you *have* to answer or act instantly. Give yourself the time you need to think through the situation, decide what you want to happen, and weigh potential consequences. If you're not ready to make a decision or give a response, say you'll get back shortly. That will give you a chance to get additional information or to consider other alternatives.

4. PRACTICE BREVITY.

Be brief or you're a bore. Learn to present any idea within sixty seconds. Don't suck the energy out of your talk with a preamble. Get right to the point. If needed, you'll fill in the background later.

5. ACKNOWLEDGE ANOTHER'S VIEW WITHOUT AGREEING TO IT.

Each person's unique background and experiences shape his or her agenda. You have a right to give your opinion; allow others the same privilege. Accepting that others think differently than you do helps you not to take affronts personally. Instead, press for their specific objections. Focus on desired consequences by thinking "results, results, results." Saying you understand that someone has a certain belief does not indicate agreement, but it does open the door for further dialogue.

6. REEVALUATE.

Ask yourself if you're expecting too much. Have you really understood what your opponent was saying? Are you too inflexible, too insistent on getting your way? Are you bypassing the real issue and potential solutions? You don't have to prove that you're right and they're wrong, but you do have to find a workable way out. Give in when something's not that important to you. Also, let those affected by the decision have a part in making it, or, at least, in submitting their ideas for consideration.

7. ASK QUESTIONS AND LISTEN VERY INTENTLY.

When people are angry, they don't want to hear your explanation (excuses, they think). They do want you to understand what they're feeling. By preparing tactful questions you give them a chance to vent before you try to reason, and you avoid hostile, defensive replies. You can probe with, "Please help me understand. . ." or "Did I hear you say that. . .?" If you fear your message isn't heard the way you meant, ask how they feel about your statement. Inquire what they're looking for to resolve a matter. Draw out their concerns and suggested solutions. What they reveal is your key to what will move them in the direction of your goal.

8. INITIATE A DIALOGUE BY TELLING HOW YOU FEEL.

Nobody knows you're unhappy unless you stand up for yourself. Factually, professionally, unemotionally, and without guilt or excuses, express your anger firmly and politely. While it's normal to want revenge, you can't think logically or creatively until you let go of your anger. Only then can you take the quantum leap, visualizing what you really want to have happen.

9. ASK FOR POLITENESS.

You have to expect respect to get it. If rudeness continues, walk away from the oversized egos, interrupters, imposers, ignorers, meeting disrupters, and other oafs. Remain polite. You don't get to be rude because others are rude to you. Try giving everyone a way out. This soothes ruffled feathers. You both keep your dignity and save face.

10. ASK THE RIGHT QUESTION, THEN WORK BACKWARDS.

A nonquestion yields no good answer. For example, "How can I impress the boss?" keeps you going around in circles. You must dig deeper. Asking, "What interests the boss that I can work on?" gives you something you can compute. Rather than getting bogged down in analyzing the problem, start with the desired result. You move from circular thinking to targeted talking when you explore what's needed to bring about an outcome you want that the other will accept.

11. WORK AT THINKING MORE CREATIVELY.

A plan inspires confidence. Having a plan is more important than the plan itself. Keep asking yourself, "What's needed in this situation?" Set aside a quiet time for creative thinking, if only a daily fifteen minutes. Be very clear about what you want as a consequence or outcome. A new idea may become clearer if you sleep on it. Turn on the faucet and utilize running water to encourage the flow of thought. Amass as many thoughts as possible without evaluating them; otherwise, you stop the flow. After that, combine similar ideas. Examine which pieces can be changed, added, or deleted to make your idea work.

12. SPEAK UP ABOUT PROBLEMS.

Tell other people what vexes you. Agree on acceptable boundaries. It's okay to express anger if your reaction is an attempt to improve the situation. Remember, even those in authority need a friend. Offer your ideas for consideration. Request what you want. It is possible to help yourself and benefit others at the same time. The acceptance or rejection is up to them, but you gain by being helpful, friendly, and respectful. So suggest new ways, limits, rules, systems, and step-by-step planning that can make it happen.

Index